Living at the Mercy Seat

Living *at the* Mercy Seat

Expositions of the Scriptures

R. C. CHAPMAN

COMMUNITY CHRISTIAN MINISTRIES
MOSCOW, IDAHO

Published by Community Christian Ministries
P.O. Box 9754, Moscow, Idaho 83843
208.883.0997 | www.ccmbooks.org

R.C. Chapman, *Living at the Mercy Seat*
Copyright © 2025 by Community Christian Ministries

Originally published in the author's lifetime as *Choice Sayings: Being Notes of Expositions of the Scriptures*.

Cover design by Samuel Dickison.
Interior design by Valerie Anne Bost.

All rights reserved. No part of this publication may be reproduced, stored in a retrieval system, or transmitted in any form by any means, electronic, mechanical, photocopy, recording, or otherwise, without prior permission of the copyright holder, except as provided by USA copyright law.

All Scripture quotations are from the King James Bible®, public. domain.

ISBN: 978-1-882840-84-7

25 26 27 28 29 30 31 32 33 34   10 9 8 7 6 5 4 3 2 1

Contents

Foreword *vii*

The Gospel *1*

The Law and the Gospel *3*

The Scriptures *5*

The Natural Man and His Religion *8*

Sin *10*

Confession of Sin *14*

Conscience *17*

The Cross of Christ *20*

Human Nature *24*

Faith *27*

Communion with God *32*

Christ *37*

Christ and the Church *39*

The Holy Spirit *43*

Christ's Example *44*

The Trial of Faith *45*

The Calling of the Church *50*

The "New Creature" *53*

Unbelief *54*

The Sins of Believers *56*

The Coming of the Lord *59*

Prayer *60*

Conflict *63*

Service *64*

Service to Christ *66*

Forgiveness *67*

Poverty of Spirit *68*

Evil Passions *70*

Self-Knowledge and Self-Judgment *71*

Humility and Self-Abasement *73*

Circumstances *75*

Strength and Continuance *78*

Character *81*

Obedience *82*

Cares *84*

Chastisement *85*

Discipline *87*

Experience *90*

A Sound Mind *91*

Danger and Temptations *92*

The Christian's Walk *93*

Trial of the Servants of Christ *96*

Dealing with the Faults of Others *97*

Evil Speaking *99*

Deep and Silent Work *100*

Little Things *102*

Fruit *103*

Christian Communion *104*

Love *107*

Justice and Judgment *109*

The Love of God *110*

The Heart and Its Deceitfulness *111*

The Form of Godliness *113*

Salvation, Justification, Pardon *114*

God's Wise and Gracious Dealings *116*

Obedience *118*

Watchfulness and Self-Denial *120*

Temptations and Falls *122*

Prayer *124*

Answers to Prayer *127*

Holiness *128*

The Secret Life and the Daily Path *129*

The Day of Small Things *130*

The Believer's Testimony to Others *131*

Happiness, Joy, Comfort, and Peace *132*

Church Discipline *134*

The Servants of the Lord *136*

Spiritual Warfare *139*

God's Deeper Dealings *140*

Pleasing the Lord *141*

Providences *143*

Gratitude *144*

Praise *145*

Foreword

"Whatever the difficulties of the times . . .
it is ever open unto us to please God."
R.C. Chapman

An ardent evangelist, a man of prayer, a man of the Word—this was Robert Cleaver Chapman. Now a little-known figure, R.C. Chapman was in his time a respected evangelist and pastor. He was a good friend of missionary Hudson Taylor and the mentor of that famous man of faith, George Müller. Charles Spurgeon called him "the saintliest man I ever knew."

Affectionately known as the Apostle of Love, Chapman was always ready to lay down his life for those around him. He regularly provided hospitality to travelers and others in need. One of his many houseguests wrote of him, "Mr. Chapman always retires at nine and rises at four . . . . He attends to the minutest bodily and spiritual wants of a stream of visitors, some of whom stay for an hour, some for a month; . . . it was his practice . . . to go round to every door and take away the boots of his guests, to clean them with his own hands."[1] As Chapman himself said, "The strength of love is shown in great things; *the tenderness of love in little things.*"[2]

1. H.B. Macartney Jr., quoted in Alexander Strauch and Robert L. Peterson, *Agape Leadership: Lessons in Spiritual Leadership from the Life of R.C. Chapman* (Littleton, CO: Lewis and Roth Publishers, 1991), 49.
2. *Living at the Mercy Seat*, 37.

The pattern of Chapman's life continually pointed away from self to his Lord. "Can I fail to praise God *always for all things*, if I have no interests but the interests of Christ, and no purposes but those of Christ?" he asked. As one biographer noted, "Robert Cleaver Chapman tried his best to be forgotten, but God intervened on our behalf."[3]

Though Chapman's humility made him reluctant to publish any of his own writings, persistent friends managed to bring some of them to the public eye. This collection was originally published under the title *Choice Sayings: Being Notes of Expositions of the Scriptures*. More than a century has passed since Robert Cleaver Chapman went to glory, but the pains and problems he addresses in these expositions remain the same. Do you need encouragement for enduring a trial? Are you troubled with worry about a problem or a fear for the future? Do you struggle with prayers that seem to keep going unanswered? Or perhaps you simply want to know what the Bible has to say about such subjects as conflict, temptation, or spiritual war. Whether your interest is academic or spiritual (beware if it is only the former—cf. James 1:22), Chapman's book is for you.

Trust in God is the most noticeable theme that weaves itself through his writing. "If we only act because our path is clear of difficulty, this is not faith," Chapman tells us. "Faith acts upon God's Word whatever the difficulty; and to walk by faith brings highest glory to God…. If we trust God, there is no limit to the power of faith, whatever the thing to be done."

---

3. Jon Bloom, "The Best Leaders Are Often Least Noticed: Robert Chapman (1803–1902)," Desiring God, January 30, 2018, https://www.desiringgod.org/articles/the-best-leaders-are-often-least-noticed.

"The best answers to prayer are those we have to wait and trust for," Chapman said. May God fill you with faith and trust as you wait upon Him.

The Editor
Moscow, Idaho
2025

The Gospel

The very first sigh on account of sin which is begotten in the heart of a sinner by the Holy Spirit is the beginning of an eternal communion with God.

Among hearers of the Gospel God remembers the sins of those only who remember not the blood of Jesus.

If God build His glory upon Christ, shall not we build on Him our hope of salvation?

Do we heartily renounce our own righteousness? And are we looking only to the atoning blood of Jesus for justification and sanctification? If so, we are poor sinners saved by grace.

The very commandment of God—"Repent"—shows a dispensation above the law, and supposes a fountain of grace in the heart of God. Were there not forgiveness with God, there could have been no commandment to repent.

As divine justice was honoured by the condemnation and cross of Christ, the Head, so is the same justice honoured by the salvation of the members.

The natural man has no apprehension of the Gospel. "What must I do?" is ever his cry. Man has done his work perfectly—that of self-destruction. He is wholly bent upon evil, altogether ruined. Hence he is a fitting object for the Gospel of God.

Unbelief is the height of presumption: it plainly proves that we are seeking for some cause of God's love in the creature, which can never be.

It is among the highest provocations the sinner can be guilty of against God, when, without the blood of Christ sprinkled on his conscience, he, in will-worship, calls God his Father.

No cup of poison so deadly as that mingled cup of law and grace, of works and faith, which is presented to men by false teachers, instead of the Gospel of the grace of God. Yet, alas, do men gladly receive, and eagerly drink, seeking to satisfy conscience!

To seek healing of soul from duties instead of the blood of Christ is taking poison to cure disease.

When we would consider the love of God in Christ, we are as one approaching the ocean: he casts a glance on the surface, but the depths he cannot sound.

The Law and the Gospel

Let a sinner look at himself in the glass of God's holiness, he must see his own condemnation; but by faith in Jesus he beholds himself free from condemnation, and stands before God in Christ as Christ Himself.

The Law was magnified by Christ, and made honourable; and therefore God in His righteousness must magnify for ever Christ and His members with Him.

Under the Law they laboured first, and rested after (Exod. 20:8-11); but under the Gospel we rest first, by faith in Jesus, and then work.

The Law begins with commands and ends with blessings; but the blessings are fruit upon lofty branches, which fallen man can never reach: he cannot and will not climb the tree. The Gospel, on the contrary, begins with promises; and promises give birth to precepts. The Law demands justice; the Gospel delights in mercy through satisfied justice. Moses blesses the law-doer; Jesus pardons the guilty and saves the lost.

Every one who hears the Gospel has a door opened to him of escape from the wrath to come. In the Day of Judgment men shall know all the past. Forgetful hearers of the Gospel shall then with gnashing of teeth remember how they once neglected so great salvation (Heb. 2:3): their worm will never die, their fire never be quenched (Mark 9:44).

No child of Adam has a right to anything from God save the wages of sin. Justice, apart from grace in Christ's cross, must allot to every sinner hell for his wages and portion. If the sinner is to have eternal life, he must have it as a free gift from God. Alas that thousands of sinners who hear the gospel will not have it, because they are too proud to be saved on God's terms of pure grace!

What is it to obey the gospel, but to believe the gospel? Unbelief says, "I will not receive Christ as a gift from God." Faith, on the contrary, says, "I want Christ in His fulness; my pinching poverty makes me glad of so rich and all-sufficient a Saviour."

The Scriptures

There are mysteries of grace and love in every page of the Bible: it is a thriving soul that finds the Book of God growing more and more precious.

A careless reader of the Scriptures never made a close walker with God.

Spread the Bible before the Lord; ask Him to teach you what *your* ignorance and what *His* wisdom.

Meditation on the Word of God is the chief means of our growth in grace: without this even prayer itself will be little better than an empty form. Meditation nourishes faith, and faith and prayer are the keys which unlock the hidden treasures of the word.

We have great need to be prepared for trials of faith and patience in so great a business as reading the Scriptures with understanding heart. It is only by faith and patience, and prayerful meditation of the Word, that we are delivered from imaginations of the flesh—from sacrificing to our own net, and burning incense to our own drag.

The laying open the heart of God is the great design of the Scriptures: happy the reader who falls in with that design!

The Bible is always a new book to those well acquainted with it.

We shall never become established in grace until we credit the Word of God as the self proving voice of Him who speaks it.

Satan has ten thousand devices for drawing us away from the Scriptures. This done, we are in his net; and, though our gracious

God put us not to shame by any outward and gross transgression, we shall become barren and unfruitful.

No believer can flourish in the ways of Christ, unless it be his custom to deal with God by the Word in the closet.

The children of God in the furnace without a good store of Scripture in their hearts are always impatient, struggling in self-will for deliverance, and thereby they do but add fuel to the fire.

If we read the Word of God chiefly to get comfort, we shall have but little, and that of doubtful kind. Let us put away this selfishness, and use the Word of God as the sword of the Spirit against the flesh in us; so will the Scriptures unfold themselves more and more, and endear Christ to us. That sword, well-handled against the flesh in ourselves, will serve us in good stead against Satan.

The Book of God is a store of manna for God's pilgrim children; and we ought to see to it that the soul get not sick and loathe the manna. The great cause of our neglecting the Scriptures is not want of time, but want of heart, some idol taking the place of Christ. Satan has been marvelously wise to entice away God's people from the Scriptures. A child of God who neglects the Scriptures cannot make it his business to please the Lord of glory: cannot make Him Lord of the conscience; ruler of the heart; the joy, portion, and treasure of the soul.

The threatenings of God's Word are designed to discourage men from their wickedness, and to drive them out of all refuges of lies to the Saviour. For the utterly self-condemned sinner there is nothing but encouragement in the whole compass of the Bible.

If it be asked, What is the proof that we digest our spiritual food?—that our knowledge of God's truth turns to growth in grace? The answer is, does it lead us into communion with God, and submission to His will? Among the marks of true communion with God, two of the plainest are a spirit of thanksgiving and a spirit of confession.

The Natural Man and His Religion

The Religion of the Natural Man is made up of pride, ignorance, and a guilty conscience: these effectually keep the sinner far from God. Grace, on the contrary, moves us to draw near to God by the blood of Jesus. It was the obedience of faith that made Abel the acceptable worshipper.

The fairest things in the world's sight are the foulest in the sight of God; to wit, the world's Wisdom and the world's Religion.

To judge by the number of creeds in the world, its Religions are many; yet there are but two—man's Religion and God's. The former ever builds on the false righteousness of the flesh; the latter on the rock Christ.

All the Religion of the Natural Man turns the Bible upside down: it begins with works, and then leads men to hope for mercy. Whereas the Bible begins with the pardon of sin, and then enjoins obedience.

Nadab and Abihu went up with Moses into the mount with God, yet afterwards perished while offering strange fire. Were natural men that profess Christ to be caught up into heaven, and sent down to earth again, they would be still but Nadabs and Abihus at enmity with God. The carnal mind must be crucified; it cannot be mended or improved.

The man who worships God without the new birth is a mocker of God, not a worshipper.

It is natural to the corrupt heart of man to deny its weakness and sinfulness, and to boast of its strength and righteousness.

If Adam in his state of uprightness could not uphold himself, how shall we, his corrupt seed, by native strength rise up out of our fall?

There are many stirrings of conscience in the Natural Man which are not grace, though often mistaken for it. Balaam, Saul, and many others, had such stirrings—conscience pulling one way and the heart another. Without grace there is no self-abhorrence, and therefore no looking to the blood of Christ. Where grace is, the soul desires deliverance from the power of sin as well as its punishment.

If you be not converted to God, you have not to be doing good works, but to learn that you can do none, and that you are to come empty to receive God's gift of eternal life by faith in Christ Jesus. Your best prayer for mercy is the true confession of your sin. Made alive in Christ, you are to bring forth fruit to God. That fruit will not be apples of Sodom or grapes of Gomorrah: such are all your good works in your natural state—your fruit will be from Jesus, the true and living vine.

Sin

The perfection of our obedience in the sight of our heavenly Father lies not so much in *attainment* as in *endeavour*. Reserves spoil obedience. We may be dealing honestly with sin that is seen outwardly, and yet not skillfully and effectually, because of not striking at the deep roots of evil within.

God indeed, as our Father in Christ Jesus, does not blame us for indwelling sin; but He does require that we should contend against it.

It is one thing to be blameless before men, and another to be aiming at that perfect obedience which Christ rendered to the Father: "I do always those things that please Him."

The first sign of spiritual life in the soul is generally the cry of distress from the sight of that which never gave trouble before—the pollution of sin. The mere natural man may dread the punishment of sin; its uncleanness he cannot feel, he cannot discern.

David said, "Horror hath taken hold upon me, because of the wicked that forsake Thy law."[1] If we be spiritually-minded, we shall in like manner mourn over the unregenerate. Lot did not apprehend as did Abraham the state of Sodom, because, without God's leading, he was in it, and, alas! too much of it.

God would ever have us regard sin in its pollution and guilt, and deal with it as done against Him (Psalm 51:4).

---

1. Psalm 119:53

Those who deny the Godhead of Christ and atonement by His blood know not their sickness; and such need not the Physician that God hath sent, nor the remedy that God hath provided.

It is a great principle of God's government, that a sin not repented of becomes a seed which greatly multiplies.

The slack conscience that questions the everlasting punishment of the ungodly betrays the soul's neglect of solemn dealing with the death of the Son of God on the tree, and of the testimonies of the scriptures thereto.

Sin does not lie in being tempted, but in not resisting temptation. The Lord Jesus Himself was tempted, and, because of His holiness, suffered pain unspeakable, yet could not be defiled. So far as we have His mind, we, His members, suffer pain in temptation; and the greater the pain of the soul the less the defilement.

How precious the words of Romans 6:10-11! "In that He died, He died unto sin once.... Likewise reckon ye also yourselves.... He liveth unto God." We with Him live to God. He died to sin by dying for sin. It was once imputed to Him. He put it away by the sacrifice of Himself; and now, with the glory of His atonement, lives at the right hand of God. The poor and needy one, by faith in the Son of God, is *in* Christ *as* Christ in God's sight. Is no sin now imputed to Christ?—so none to the believer. Is Christ, with the glory of His atonement, accepted of God?—so the believer. The apprehending by faith these great things is the true way of mortifying sin. "Sin shall not have dominion over you; for ye are not under the law, but under grace" (v. 14).

The sinner thinks to improve himself by lopping off this or that branch of his sin; he knows not that thereby he does but nourish the evil root.

The greater power we have over sin, the more intolerable do we feel the burden of it, and the more earnestly do we seek the cleansing of that blood which purges the conscience from its defilement.

Let us not be discouraged by any humiliating discoveries we may make of the evils of our hearts. God knows them all, and has provided the blood of Jesus Christ His Son to cleanse us from all sin.

God regards our sins with the heart of a father, but not with the eye of a judge; for his sin-avenging justice has no further demands: the cross made satisfaction.

The imaginations of man's heart are only evil continually. Oh to come to close quarters with this truth! to be willing to be judged by it! There must be something more than man's own will for this; there must be the working of the Spirit of God.

We little know the deep mysteries of the human heart: it is because of our deep sin and pride that we bear correction with so much impatience; but if we had a dangerous malady, and knew it, we should not complain of the bitter taste and troublesome effects of the medicine given us to heal our disease.

Romans 8:13-14.[2] *One* blow will sometimes take the life of the body; but to mortify sin we must be *always* striking, because sin is always struggling.

If we contend with sin, be assured that we shall be victorious sooner or later: there is not a single sin but the defiling power thereof may be subdued (1 John 1:7).[3]

---

2. "For if ye live after the flesh, ye shall die: but if ye through the Spirit do mortify the deeds of the body, ye shall live. For as many as are led by the Spirit of God, they are the sons of God."
3. "But if we walk in the light, as he is in the light, we have fellowship one with another, and the blood of Jesus Christ his Son cleanseth us from all sin."

The so-called innocent amusements of the world are only contrivances to forget God.

It is the nature of sin to obtain great power by little beginnings.

Confession of Sin

Soon as the word is uttered, "I have sinned," that very moment flies the seraph (Isa. 6). God "is faithful and just to forgive us our sins." When we confess them in the name of Jesus, justice, having been satisfied by the blood of Christ, is swift to pardon.

God cannot seal a pardon in the soul without confession (Psalm 32:3, 5).[4]

As we practise confession, so will be our happiness and joy; for all true confession is followed by the spirit of praise.

If in coming to God we complain against ourselves, let us thank Him that we have a heart to complain.

The Spirit of God never heals save as He wounds; and if those seeking Christ have not peace, it is because there is still in them some remnant of fancied goodness. Tell out the whole heart to God, and the conscience will be cleansed by confessing sin over the head of the scapegoat.

There is a counterfeit confession of sin; let us beware of this counterfeit. We may be sure the sorrow is not deep if the sin be not subdued.

If so be we are ready in the confession of our faults, and have faith in the blood of sprinkling, those very faults will serve our growth in grace: they will be like manure to the field or garden.

---

4. "When I kept silence, my bones waxed old through my roaring all the day long . . . . I acknowledge my sin unto thee, and mine iniquity have I not hid. I said, I will confess my transgressions unto the Lord; and thou forgavest the iniquity of my sin. Selah."

God kills to make alive. He smites men's consciences to make them judge themselves. The first great step when a man desires to be saved is unqualified self-condemnation. Sin unconfessed is imputed; but sin confessed is blotted out by God. The sinner, coming in the name of Jesus, has a *title* to life: the ground of that title is the very name and justice of God.

We should confess to God every inward evil as soon as it is discovered to us: and if we have trespassed against our brother, to Him also we should speedily make confession. By so doing we shall keep up the communion of love with God and with each other.

It was the imputation of our sins to Christ that hid from Him the face of God the Father. It is our unconfessed disobedience that brings a cloud between Christ and us.

When on entering a house I see a child in disgrace for disobedience, although I tenderly consider the erring child, I especially feel with the grieved, sorrowing parent. When we sin, and are chastened of God, we should rather consider how the heart of our heavenly Father has by us been grieved, than be taken up with the smart of our stripes by His rod of correction.

If we practise the true confession of sin, and so cease to grieve the Holy Spirit of God, we shall have the testimony of the Spirit that the ear, thumb, and toe are tipped with blood and oil.

Keep no secrets from God. Confession of sin to Him in all detail will greatly help us in the subduing it.

The sinful thought of the heart is, in the sight of God, the act: evils in life always proceed from evils nourished in the heart.

Do we think that God is pleased with shallow confessions of deep sins? Compare Job 40:4 with 42:2-6. "Behold, I am vile; what shall I answer thee? I will lay mine hand upon my mouth." "I know that thou canst do every thing, and that no thought can be withholden from thee. Who is he that hideth counsel without knowledge? therefore have I uttered that I understood not; things too wonderful for me, which I knew not. Hear, I beseech thee, and I will speak: I will demand of thee, and declare thou unto me. I have heard of thee by the hearing of the ear: but now mine eye seeth thee. Wherefore I abhor myself, and repent in dust and ashes."

After we have been able, by the grace of God, to subdue any besetting sin, and it seems to be dead, let us still be confessing to God that it is within us. By thus doing we shall show that we are not living on the victory but on God Himself. Indwelling sin will be thus regarded by the eye of our Father rather as our sickness than our fault.

All unconfessed sin has power over us; but all confessed sin God helps us to subdue: He will never blame us for sins confessed.

The speediest confession is the easiest and the best.

Conscience

When peace reigns in the conscience there is always power over sin. Peace is like a sentinel that keeps guard at the door of the heart; if the sentinel be off his post, either the tumult within drowns the voice of the Spirit, or, because of the stillness of death, his voice is not heard.

A guilty conscience is one of Satan's great weapons against the children of God: faith can only be bold as the conscience is clean.

There is no trial to the believer like guilt upon the conscience; but it is the triumph of faith to see guilt removed by the atoning blood of Christ. A very little stain upon the conscience makes a wide breach in our communion with God.

If we have a doubt upon our minds upon any point, we should go straight to Jesus to get it solved. Love abhors a winding course.

If the conscience be not rightly instructed, it becomes a tool for Satan; if it speaks a false peace, it works ruin; and if it does not speak peace at all, it is a tormentor.

We should never deal lightly with the whispers of a doubtful conscience.

Let Christ keep the heart, and the heart shall keep the life.

Our lack of walking in the Spirit often moves others to like negligence.

How great a blessing is a tender conscience; one that will discern and deal with a little sin—that will lead us to say, "Search me, O God!" In this state we not only grieve at an angry thought, or an outbreak of temper, but even for a thought of unbelief that may but glance across the mind.

The pardon of sin sealed on the conscience strengthens the soul for communion with God; whilst guilt on the conscience drives us from God. These are noiseless things in the world, but great things with God.

The child of God should remember that he has the root of every evil within him: if he take not heed to tend the garden of his conscience, evil weeds will spring up and grow; especially will the besetting sins of his unconverted days be his plague.

A scrupulous conscience comes of the flesh, and ignorance of God's will; but a good conscience is among the best of God's blessings, for it is cleansed by the blood of Christ, and enlightened by the scriptures and the Spirit of God.

We must deal with our consciences as people do with their houses: if they would keep their dwellings clean, they must day by day be cleaning.

A spiritual conscience deals most with the evil of the heart; but when the conscience is not spiritual, the heart is the last thing dealt with.

A rebuke from the Lord duly regarded will lead us into safe paths, whilst a rebuke not heeded is the forerunner of sharp correction.

The heavenly conscience never says, "*Must* I give up this? *Must* I give up that?" for this pleases not the heart of Christ.

Have I faith and a good conscience? Then I can leave everything to God—let Him give, or take, or withhold as He pleases.

A pure conscience is a conscience so thoroughly purged by the blood of Christ that it makes the soul, as it were, a mirror wherein is seen the face of our heavenly Father.

A tender conscience concerning unbelief and its slightest stirrings will greatly help us in our path of obedience and in our walk with God.

We ought to be ever trying our consciences by the Word of God, and helping our neighbours to do the same. It would indeed be a blessing to the saints, were they to exercise themselves in judging everything by the Scriptures. A child of God may walk unblameably in men's eyes, yet have little of the mind of Christ, and little of the spirit of communion: his conscience may be in so small a measure guided by the word of God that as to edifying others he is little better than a piece of lumber.

The Cross of Christ

The cross of Christ is the life of all true communion with God, and those who draw nearest to God best know the mystery of that cross.

If the sufferings of Christ, who humbled Himself and became obedient unto death—the death of the cross—be much in my heart, I shall see my worst enemy to be pride, especially pride of wisdom, and pride of righteousness. I shall charge my soul, as did the king of Syria his captains: "Fight neither with small nor great, save only with the king of Israel."[5] In my soul's warfare let pride be subdued, and every other sin is held in chains.

It is the secret of the prevention and cure of all evil to begin, and go through, each day, with the cross of Christ (John 6:56).[6]

The precepts of Scripture are given to guide the life of a Christian, and their claims are all founded on the cross of Christ.

In the cross of Christ is life; in the way of His precepts, liberty. Let us take up every cross that lies in our way—cut off the right hand and pluck out the right eye: the blessing *must* come down.

By the cross of Christ the world is crucified to us, and we are crucified to the world; whilst we, through the Spirit, are mortifying the deeds of the body, we are gaining by all our losses, and have good success even by that which the flesh accounts bitter disappointment.

There is virtue in the name of Christ to make this vale of tears a fruitful, pleasant place.

---

5. 1 Kings 22:31
6. "He that eateth my flesh, and drinketh my blood, dwelleth in me, and I in him."

He who most walks in fellowship with God has the deepest and truest apprehension of Christ. Such a one will love to consider how He who was in the form of God emptied Himself of His state of pure equality with God; how the Word made flesh, at every step of His humiliation, above all on the cross, made manifest His glory. Of all the works of God, redemption is the greatest. It is only in the cross of our Lord Jesus Christ that the perfections of God are fully manifested; and of that cross we can have no true understanding, save by the Holy Scriptures and by the Holy Spirit of God.

When the Son of God had taken on Him the form of a servant, He could say, "My Father is greater than I"[7]; but His obedience showed Him to be equal with God: obedience unto the death of the cross was such as only the Son of God could be called unto, and only He could render.

From the sixth to the ninth hour there was darkness over the land; darkness at noonday. In the proper natural course of the love of God the Father towards His Son, the Father's countenance must have been ever lifted up on the Lord Jesus; but Christ was the surety of the better covenant, and God must deal as a sin-revenging judge with His own Son on the cross as our surety and sin-bearer: "Cursed is every one that hangeth on a tree."[8] The land is a type of Christ; and while from the sixth to the ninth hour, the course of the old creation was suffering, in regard to the land, strange and awful interruption, even thick darkness at noon, thereby was

7. John 14:28
8. Gal. 3:13

shown forth the greatest work, the greatest event of the new creation; God not sparing His own Son, but delivering Him up for us all; Christ who knew no sin made sin for us, that we might be made the righteousness of God in Him; Christ made a curse for us, to redeem us from the curse of the law. The mind of the Lord Jesus was at every moment one with the mind of God the Father; but the Lord's obedience grew with growing trial, and according to demand upon Him: it was on the cross that He obeyed to the uttermost; on the cross He made manifest to the full His oneness of mind with the Father. Now He dieth no more; as having once been crucified, and as having glorified the Father on the earth, He dwells forever in the bosom of the Father, in the light of His countenance. By faith we dwell with Christ the Lord, and learn a little of His cross: at the resurrection we shall learn indeed; yet evermore be learning—and evermore be praising the Lamb that was slain. Be it then ever present with us in our sojourn here, that Christ, through the eternal Spirit, *offered Himself* without spot to God. So shall our hearts be full of the song, "Holy, holy, holy, is the Jehovah of hosts!" (Isaiah 6:3).

Christ's *work* is the light, life, joy, glory, and perfume of heaven.

There is no testimony to God's hatred of sin like the cross of Christ. There are testimonies thereto above, around, and beneath us; but in the cross, and that only, we see to the full God's hatred of sin.

Christ *descended* lower and lower, even to the depths of the cross; but in God's sight it was a perpetual ascent to the throne of glory.

If with godly sorrow we would grieve for sin, we must regard it in fellowship with Christ in the light of the cross.

The law of nature, the law of Moses, and a corrupted gospel, are so many refuges of lies which men flee to for salvation, instead of coming to the cross of Christ.

The cross of Christ is the meeting-place for God and the sinner. It is the meeting-place of God with His people. It is also the meeting-place of saints with one another: it is only as Jesus crucified dwells in the midst of them that they can meet each other to profit.

Mercy to Christ, my Surety, would have been death eternal to me.

In the cross of Christ the holiness of God is perfectly revealed: such is His holiness that the heavens are not clean in His sight.

The Scriptures show us that it is by the cross of Christ God bears with the ungodly. The justice of God is so magnified by that cross that it can delight in longsuffering towards the unregenerate; one great end of this longsuffering is the calling out of the church.

All the trials and all the sufferings of all creatures—were they heaped together—must not be compared with Christ's sufferings on the cross.

As the sin-avenging God of holiness and justice, God forsook Christ on the cross; but He was infinitely well-pleased with Christ and His death of atonement. God accepted the work of His beloved Son, and in token of that acceptance, raised Him from the dead.

Human Nature

The carnal mind ever lies in wait for self-exaltation, and will catch at any straw for this end.

Deceptions are recorded in God's Word with their corrections, that we may avoid them: if Abraham deceived, we find him corrected; if Isaac deceived, he is rebuked; and the deception Jacob practised on his father was visited upon him for almost all his life. If David and Jonathan had agreed to cast themselves only upon God, how much after-trouble would have been prevented! (1 Sam. 20 and on).

Correction does not always consist in bitter things coming upon us, but it may be in our failing to obtain some higher honour, which, had we walked in greater simplicity, we should have received from God.

That is the hardest to bear which touches my pride; offended pride has no bowels, and hearkens to no reason.

Hurry is the working of the flesh; faith, like God, works at leisure.

Angels have no envy, because they have no pride. Is God glorified? Angels are happy. Let the glory of God be our delight, our meat, our drink. Love envieth not: if one member be honoured, saith love, that is my honour, my joy.

Christ must be extolled and be very high in our hearts, if the unruly flesh and its wayward cravings are to be curbed.

Self-righteousness and carnal wisdom are ringleaders of the enemies of the soul.

We should deal with our corrupt nature as we would with a notorious thief—never trust it.

The greater part of our sorrows arise from mortified pride, thwarted self-will, and anxious unbelief.

Pride has always an envious eye and an envious tongue: envy is but the vexation of pride.

It is a mark of true growth in grace and spirituality of mind to be looking back and dealing afresh with God respecting past iniquities. The soul is greatly profited by a tender conscience dealing before the Lord with the sins of *early youth*. Defects of character and feeble resistance of temptation may be traced up to neglect of dealing with God through the cross about our easily besetting sins. Looking back and reviewing our past state will enable us to read the story of God's present discipline and aid us in the present and future growth of our souls.

The gospel of Christ is a more open enemy to the pride of man than is the law of Moses. Israel received Moses' commandments with vows of obedience, but said of Christ, "Away with Him! Crucify Him!"

The master-sin of man is independence of God. What is the cure? Christ the Son of God self-abased, even to the death of the cross (Phil. 2:5-8).

Naaman, the Syrian, was somebody in his own sight; therefore he was angry at the commandment which made him nothing.

If we think we are undervalued, let us weigh ourselves in God's balances, and we shall easily bear the slight.

The vauntings of self-exalting man are but the trickery of his pride, to hide his native vanity from his own eye and his neighbour's.

Man without God may seem something at a distance. Come near him; be familiar with him, you find him to be nothing. But "blessed are they that dwell in Thy house; they will be still praising Thee."[9] Even now, while yet in the earthly house of this tabernacle, we find that growing acquaintance with God brings with it increase of reverence and love. Oh, blessed hope! We shall know as we are known; see face to face and be satisfied; waking up in the likeness of the Lord.

Many there are who can talk well of the truth of the gospel, but who, when called to self-denial, taking up crosses, suffering for Christ's sake, prove sounding brass and tinkling cymbals: knowledge puffeth up, but love edifieth.

Absalom's vanity let his hair grow long; and his long hair did the service of the hangman's rope. Let parents hear the warning voice, and teach their children from earliest days to reckon the fear of God their best ornament.

---

9. Psalm 84:4

Faith

If we act only because our path is clear of difficulty, this is not faith. Faith acts upon God's Word whatever the difficulty; and to walk by faith brings highest glory to God; but it is a crucifying the flesh.

To be strong in faith two things are needful—a very low esteem of ourselves, and a very high esteem of Christ.

The chief excellency of faith is that it brings us into fellowship with God. Abel—the first spoken of in Hebrews 11—is commended, not because of any great deed in man's account, but because he worshipped God acceptably. Nevertheless, if we trust God, there is no limit to the power of faith, whatever the thing to be done.

God shelters the weak in faith from many a storm, whereby the strong in faith must be proved (Gen. 22).

When a man builds house or ship, he takes heed that no beam be strained; so God never overtaxes our faith, but brings in comfort, knowing our frame, not suffering us to have sorrow upon sorrow, according to Philippians 2:27.[10]

By neglect of God, and forgetfulness of His word and promise, our minds may become blinded to plainest things. Isaac, through self-will and allowing his natural partiality to blind him, would have set aside as nothing the purposes of God concerning Jacob.

---

10. "For indeed he was sick nigh unto death: but God had mercy on him; and not on him only, but on me also, lest I should have sorrow upon sorrow."

When we are especially strong in faith, we have especial need to watch against unbelief (compare 1 Sam. 26:5 and on, with 27:1) for as the flesh takes great occasion by sin, so by grace; and no one who studies much that profitable book, his own heart, but must know it.

Soon after Abraham had greatly trusted God, he through unbelief denied his wife. Moses, the meekest of men, spake unadvisedly with his lips. David, the humble, forgiving man, was moved to proud wrath by the words of Nabal.

Faith, which always acts according to the mind of Christ, stoops to no unworthy device for deliverance from trial, leaving consequences wholly with God.

A little increase of faith works great changes of judgment in us, and brings forth the otherwise hidden riches of the grace and wisdom of God: it stirs His power to do wonders for us, dividing the sea when the waves thereof roar.

Hebrews 11:24—Moses' first great step of faith was the refusing to be called the son of Pharaoh's daughter. Yet Moses mistook the time for delivering Israel by forty years. He was too hasty; right in point of purpose, not in point of time. He was not content with the bare doing the will of God; he would straightway accomplish some great thing. After leaving Pharaoh's house he should have asked of God further guidance. We need guidance step by step. "I (saith the Lord) taught Ephraim to go, taking them by their arms" (Hosea 11:3).

Faith looks straight to the command in order to obey it, and takes the promise for her support. She pushes on her way, regardless of dangers. Moses must "go forward," though the next step lead the people into the sea. Whatever appearances may say to us, it is by advancing in the narrow way of obedience that we prove the truth of the promises; and the faithfulness, the wisdom, and the power of our promise-giving God.

We must not be deceived by appearances, but be sustained by promises. When Jacob looked upon Joseph's coat, which had been brought to him, he should have said, "I *see* the coat that is covered with blood; I *hear* the report of the death of Joseph; but, Lord, I *believe* Thy word—Thy promises concerning the greatness and the glory of my son: what Thou hast spoken Thou wilt perform."

It is a great proof of the strength and steadiness of faith when, diligent in pleasing God, we rise above our obedience to God Himself.

Grace makes light of sacrifices, because of looking straight to Jesus.

Unbelief begets all sorts of evils; faith prevents and cures them.

Would that the saints of God tried themselves by this test: "How much do I believe?" instead of "How much do I know?"

We please God by trusting Him; trusting His grace, His love, His wisdom; trusting without limit: but it is only by little and little that we come to account our own wisdom folly, and God's wisdom true wisdom—*wisdom infinite*; then we are able to yield up ourselves unreservedly unto Him.

Faith labours, and holds on, despite of all appearances, and in the midst of all difficulties.

Rather let us look by faith to Christ at God's right hand, than at the mountain of difficulties before our eyes.

One of the best answers to prayer is to be able to continue in prayer (see Matt. 15:21-28).

Faith perpetually cries to God for its own increase.

All things that are within the compass of God's promises are within the compass of faith.

Let faith lay heart-sins upon Christ, and there will be no plague-spots upon the skin.

Faith waits upon God; but she waits also for God. Jacob (in Gen. 32:9-12) waited upon God regarding Esau his brother; but he did not wait for God. Had he done so, he would not have bowed down (33:3) seven times to his brother: Esau must have bowed down to him (27:29).

God delights in putting faith to do that which the flesh declares impossible. Oh, how precious a jewel is that resolute faith which walks with God under all circumstances, wrestling against the powers of darkness, making no bow to the Haman of evil customs, or evil principles!

We cannot be losers by trusting God, for He is honoured by faith, and most honoured when faith discerns His love and truth behind a thick cloud of His ways and providence. Happy those who are thus tried! Thus saith the Lord, "Count it all joy when ye fall into divers temptations" (James 1:2). Let us only be clear of unbelief and a guilty conscience, and we shall hide ourselves in the rock and pavilion of the Lord, sheltered beneath the wings of everlasting love till all calamities be overpast.

Faith can bear the test of death and burial, and can sing praises to God under any circumstances.

A steadfast purpose to trust God, when He seems to unbelief to be breaking promise, betokens a growth in faith. "Though He slay me, yet will I trust in Him" (Job 13:15).

God often encourages the weak in faith by giving speedy answers to prayer; but the strong in faith will be tested by God's delays.

The prayer of self-will may get its answer, as with the Israelites: "He gave them their request, but sent leanness into their soul" (Psalm 106:15).

Faith is the good cable that, stretched and strained, does not break in the storm.

Trial humbles the soul and enables it to bear the ripened blessing, and to carry a full cup with a steady hand. Faith is not discouraged, but holds on in patience, expecting the promised blessing in the fitting time.

What is the food and nourishment of faith? "My flesh is meat indeed, and My blood is drink indeed" (John 6:55).

To take God at His word is the business of faith.

Faith can never fail of the reward of perseverance: the Lord delights in persevering faith.

In trial of faith, let us take heed to our spirit that we trust God without stint. The soul's repose in Him is His delight; and He will honour it. Jehovah sitteth King upon the floods, and faith sits with Him.

Communion with God

God, in His dealings with His froward children, shows the forbearance of His love; but it is with the obedient that He walks in the fellowship of His love. In both cases He gets glory to Himself. Happy are they who live under His smile of approbation.

Fellowship with the Father, and with His Son Jesus Christ, and the communion of the Spirit, should be the daily household bread to our souls.

Unless the great truths of God's eternal purpose of grace, and His electing love, occupy their due place in our hearts, we must of necessity, more or less, misapprehend all truth: we can neither fulfil our obligations to God nor even duly discern them.

If we come forth from the closet of communion, the atmosphere of evil speaking will be to us as the tainted air of some great city to one that has been breathing the pure air of a mountaintop, or the fresh breezes of the seashore.

Unless our souls are living in communion with God, the scriptures will not yield us their strength and nourishment.

There is nothing so teaching as *walking* with God; nothing so sifting to the heart and conscience as seeking in all things to walk before Him; to hear, to speak, and to act for one great end, namely, to please God, and to do His will from the heart.

The Lord guides us with His eye; that is, He will so guide us, as to assure us of His guidance. He will deal with us as a tender mother with her little ones, who suffers them not out of her sight.

There is no fellowship with God, but through the blood of His dear Son. It is by this He speaks to us, and calls us children; and by it we cry, "Abba, Father," pouring out our hearts into His bosom. And we can speak to Him as we cannot speak to human ear, because the heart of man is not as the heart of God.

We can never thrive except we seek God in secret; and if we begin in our closets we shall not end there, we shall also seek and find Him in the assemblies of the saints.

It is one of the blessed fruits of the habit of walking with God, that the soul knows what to do when it has displeased God. "A wounded spirit who can bear?"[11] Yet, even that burden God can enable us to cast upon Him.

When Abraham first set foot on his pilgrimage, he knew not what meetings with God were laid up for him: he ventured on the bidding and promise of God, and his mercies multiplied on him as he advanced.

Whenever we are living *before man* instead of walking *before God*, there will be restlessness and disquietude.

It is impossible for God to meet His saints in the way of fellowship, except in the path of obedience. When they are out of that path, He meets them with correction, in order to bring them into fellowship with Himself.

If we see the least trace of the mind of Christ in anyone, we should remember that in such the heart of God delights.

Carelessness about the friendship of Christ is the crying sin of the church.

When we say, "Lord, bring us near to Thyself," we pray for many things, which, when they come, will be bitter to our

---

11. Proverbs 18:14

taste. At such times it is well to remember our Forerunner: He asked to be glorified; but before heaven was opened to Him and He received therein, He had to pass through the garden of Gethsemane, and on the cross to cry, "My God, my God, why hast Thou forsaken me?"

It ought to be a grievous thing to us to have a wish, however slight, contrary to the mind of Christ.

As soon as it is our *settled purpose* to please Christ, He takes us for His bosom friends.

The more we have of Christ in our hearts, the less room for self.

How sweetly, how pleasantly, may a Christian beguile his way to glory, by casting all his burden of sin and care upon Jesus, and walking in love and fellowship with Him all the day long! He who casts his burdens upon the Lord walks lightly and happily, as one who has no burden at all.

Communion with Christ can only be kept up by constant watchfulness. Where there is much love between friends, a cold look is matter of complaint. Let us be very jealous over ourselves for the Lord; watching against the least shyness between the soul and Christ. Keep up constant intercourse with Him; be quick and dexterous in taking small matters to Him; and the fruit will be growth of communion.

Though in a season of temptation we may see nothing in ourselves but what is vile and hateful, our very struggles of love after Christ betoken His Spirit dwelling within us.

If we would have experience of the sympathy of the Lord Jesus, we must be much at His cross, and be much occupied with the sorrows of others.

There is a short road to comfort in affliction that few of God's people tread; it is to be thinking much more of Christ's blessedness than of our own sorrow; but, alas! sympathy is for the most part all on *one* side. Christ has perfect sympathy with us. Oh that we had fellowship with Him in His joy at the right hand of God!

Though Christ can be grieved at a thousand things in us that no eye but His can see, yet none so easily pleased as He by our little endeavours of love.

Our joy in Christ speaks a language that all hearts can understand, and is a testimony for Him, such as mere knowledge and utterance can never give.

It is but a small proof of love to visit a friend who lives next door, but to go to a distance over hill and dale bespeaks love indeed. Let us show our love to Christ, by sparing no pains, no labour, in order to seek Him in prayer, in reading the word, and in meditation thereon. Let us joyfully surmount all difficulties, and joyful communion will be our recompense.

If we do anything without taking counsel of God, we—to speak of Him after the manner of men—hide the matter from Him our Father, and so grieve His Spirit. We do Him wrong, and ourselves also, if in anything we have not fellowship with Him.

When it is whispered by the Spirit of God, that He who is at God's right hand would be honoured if we do such a thing, or if we do it not—if we disregard the still small voice, although we may not be put to open shame, we shall miss the smile of approval so precious to the obedient child.

The cause of lack of communion with God is summed up in this—disobedience. Another may take away my substance, or my life, but cannot spoil me of my communion with God; if I lack this, I am myself the thief and the robber.

We ought to be always happy in God, and in His ways; if we are not, we mar the quality of our obedience.

We are never so well prepared for effectual service to man as when we are holding fellowship with God.

Let us be skillful to make God's matters ours: then shall we see that He makes our matters His.

Those who know what it is to deal much with God know that their hopes and desires must, as it were, be buried, and that they must leave it with Him to bring about a resurrection in His own time and way.

God measures out His communion of love according to diligence in seeking Him.

It is well for us to shut up our desires within the compass of trusting and pleasing God.

If our fellowship be with the Father and His dear Son, we shall know from the character of our Father what are His wishes. Errors in judgment spring more or less from lack of fellowship with Him. Acquaintance with His heart of love will enlarge ours.

We have access to God with boldness and confidence through Jesus, the Son of the Father. Do we tell out our tale at the throne of grace? Fellowship signifies the opening the heart on both sides, and that without reserve.

Christ

Christ twice passed the angels by. He sank far below them in His humiliation; He rose far above them in His exaltation.

If Christ be the life and beauty of our days of sunshine, so is He the brother born for our adversity; and His love shall gild and strike through the darkest cloud. Having been once a sufferer, He communes with His suffering members, and instructs us to put our trials into a just balance; to call our affliction light and momentary (2 Cor. 4:17-18).[12]

Resting wholly on Christ; ceasing wholly from the works of the flesh—is the secret of abiding in Him.

Growing acquaintance with Christ makes Him more and more precious to our souls. If Christ were anything less than unsearchable, He could not satisfy us—could neither fill the heart, nor give peace to the conscience.

The strength of love is shown in great things; the tenderness of love in little things. Christ showed the strength of His love on the cross by dying and bearing the curse for us; the tenderness of His love when He said, "Behold My mother!" "Children, have ye any meat?" "Woman, why weepest thou?"

There was an immeasurable difference between the state of Christ on the cross when He said, under the terrors of the Judge,

---

[12]. "For our light affliction, which is but for a moment, worketh for us a far more exceeding and eternal weight of glory; while we look not at the things which are seen, but at the things which are not seen: for the things which are seen are temporal; but the things which are not seen are eternal."

"My God, my God, why hast Thou forsaken Me?" and when He said, "Father, into Thy hands I commend My Spirit."

"Let this mind be in you, which was also in Christ Jesus" (Phil. 2:5). He could not sink lower than His cross: we can no more fathom the depths of His humiliation than comprehend the glory of His Godhead. His exaltation answers to His cross. He cannot rise higher than the right hand of God, nor find sweeter resting-place from His sufferings and His toil than the bosom of the Father. His rest and exaltation we must share, being joint-heirs with Christ; nor will He be satisfied until His members be seated with Him on His throne. Then let this mind rule and reign in us which reigned in Christ Jesus (see Phil. 2:5-15); and since the humble mind, hard of attainment, must needs go before honour from God, let us be thankful for all God's discipline, however bitter, without which pride will not stoop, nor vain man come to knowledge of himself.

May the fulness of Christ replenish our enlarged hearts day by day. By communion with Him the soul grows more and more capacious, and yet acquaintance with Him makes us feel more and more our own littleness.

Let it be our habit to feed daily upon Christ in secret; thus shall we eat and drink, discerning the Lord's body, in the assembly for the supper of the Lord.

Would we be filled with love towards Christ—let us consider Christ's love towards us in the death of the cross.

Christ and the Church

"How precious, also, are Thy thoughts unto me, O God! How great is the sum of them!" (Psalm 139:17). This is the language of Christ, the Head, regarding the members as one with Himself. The Epistle to the Ephesians is the beating out of this piece of gold.

Never take a winding path to look for acceptance with God—go straight to Christ; but when you would look at the children of God, look well at *Christ first*, and then see the saints in Him.

Christ calls Himself the Husband of His Church, because the bond of marriage is the closest and tenderest of all human ties; and to show the purity of His love, He calls her at the same time His sister. His tenderness delights to take occasion by the infirmities of His spouse. She leans on Him, not only for support, protection, and guidance, but also and chiefly for communion; and leaning is melted into adoring love, which is to Him as spiced wine. He sees His own image in the Church, and this is among His chief joys.

It was the Bridegroom who bare the sins of His spouse in His own body on the tree. What other burden will He not bear? Even the troubles that our own folly brings upon us are occasions to His love, if we do but cast the burden upon Him; but if we do not judge ourselves, He knows how to chasten us to bring us to self-judgment, that He may comfort His mourners with His immeasurable grace and love.

The lonely, the mournful, the friendless, the tempted, the dejected, the despised, the forsaken, the outcast, Christ will wait on each one of them, whatever his case, as though that one were His only charge. By this exact and special oversight of each member of His body, how precious, how lovely, how glorious, does Christ appear!

If Christ will not be satisfied with His present glory at the right hand of God without having His Church, the members of His body, with Him, how can we be content without Him in this valley of the shadow of death, this present evil world?

The candlestick in the temple was a type of the Church. It was for the high priest to supply the oil, to trim the lamp, to watch and tend it; the light must be ever brightly burning.

The ruin of a kingdom is a little thing in God's sight, in comparison with division among a handful of sinners redeemed by the blood of Christ.

When the body is in perfect health, there is a noiseless, perfect cooperation of the members; so was it with the church at Pentecost, and so it ought to be with us now.

To reform the Church of God we should always begin with self-reform. Schisms and divisions will increase so long as we begin with reforming others. Wisdom is only with the lowly.

Every kind of self-pleasing is rebuked and put down in the 2nd of Philippians; but, alas! the Church of God in these days is more like the carnal, puffed up, schismatic Corinthians than the lowly saints at Philippi, whose fellowship in the Spirit made glad the heart of Paul.

The new creation is God's delight; of that new creation Christ is the Head; as one with the Church Christ stands before God.

The Church, the body of Christ, cannot rise above its present low estate, until there be a conscience in the members of fulfilling each one his office in the body.

While I mourn over schisms and divisions in the Church of God, I justify God and bless Him for the wisdom and equity of His discipline: He gives us to reap as we sow.

The titles given to the Church in Scripture bespeak heavenly unity, such as "the body," "the vine," "temple of God," "a holy nation," "a chosen generation," "a royal priesthood." Such words set forth the church of God as a witness for Him in the world; but the names which have been invented by men are names of sects, and declare our shame.

The Church of God is a field that needs double ploughing.

Christ ever enjoys perfect communion with His Father; He craves also communion with us His members (Rev. 3:20); and when this is denied Him by our ways of selfishness, He turns to the Father, and finds joy and rest in communion with Him. The mourners in the Church of God over its low estate must in like manner betake themselves to the Father and the Son, for fellowship by the Spirit, when they cannot find what their hearts long after among their brethren.

The ark of God at Jordan went before the people—was in their midst—followed after. Christ is the leader, the rereward,[13] and the glory in the midst of the Church; their life, and bond of fellowship.

As Christ is the brightness of the glory of the Father, so is the Church the brightness of Christ's glory. He, as the Sun of righteousness, sheds forth, through the church, the beams of His light.

As without Christ the perfections of the Father were not manifested, so the glory of Christ was not shown until His body the Church, which is His fulness, was manifested. But the Church

---

13. Obsolete spelling of *rearward*, a military rear guard.

does not shine by native excellency; she is made up of those who, being by nature vile and of the earth, are created anew by the Spirit of God. The life, beauty, and glory of the Church are all from Christ her Lord derived. Whereas Christ is by nature the brightness of the Father's glory.

The Holy Spirit

How sure a teacher is the Spirit of Truth! He "searcheth all things, yea, the deep things of God" (1 Cor. 2:10). He comprehends the love of Christ, which passeth knowledge, and all the windings of the heart of man. He is the Paraclete within us, pleading for Christ with our heart, printing the name of Jesus on its fleshly tables, and causing us to increase in the knowledge of God. We never give up what by His anointing we have once embraced; it is graven on the heart as with the point of a diamond.

The Spirit of God, who is of one mind with Christ, the Son of God, dwells in believers by virtue of their oneness with Christ; and, although so often grieved, will never give up to destruction any one, even the weakest, of Christ's members.

God always dwells by His Holy Spirit in His people. Let us be careful not to grieve this glorious Paraclete. Let us be looking continually at the blood of Christ and watch against little trespasses, little breaches of love, suspicions, rash censures, and coldness of heart.

By the mere natural understanding men may learn much of the truth of God, but afterwards renounce and deny it. If by the Spirit's unction we learn anything, we hold it fast. His true teaching carries with it assurance to the soul that it is God's truth we are learning. Of this assurance Satan has his counterfeit, and only by walking humbly with God shall we detect the fraud.

Christ's Example

"He that saith he abideth in Him, ought himself also so to walk, even as He walked" (1 John 2:6). Christ's example is our rule. It is to the Christian what imperial weights and measures are to men of traffic: from that standard there is no appeal.

It is not in every *act* of the blessed Lord that we should follow Him; but the mind of Christ is always our pattern. Instance: His forty days' fasting. His precepts will guide us to discern His mind in considering His acts.

Adam, by creation God's servant, brake away from the yoke: Christ, the Son of God, took on Him the servant's form.

The children of God cannot grow in the knowledge of their own hearts, unless they be accustomed to set the example of Christ before their inward eye. We ought to try our spirits, aims, thoughts, and desires by the example of Christ. If we do this, we shall discern the current of self-willed pride running through our corrupt nature. A great discovery!

The Saviour was especially pleasing to God when He was dumb, and opened not His mouth—doing nothing, only suffering the will of God. It is well with us when treading in our Master's steps.

The child of God proves the strength and grace of His heavenly Father only as he walks in the ways of the Lord Jesus Christ.

The Trial of Faith

We are to distinguish between trial of faith and chastisement: in the former case we readily bow, and bring forth fruits of grace; but if we be rebellious, we are under correction.

Paul's thorn in the flesh was God's gift to preserve him from pride, although it was the messenger of Satan to buffet him. Thus God uses the Wicked One for our profit, for the glory of His all-sufficient grace, and for the Tempter's confusion.

Our trials are needful now for the exercise and growth of faith, and no less needful for our joy and glory at the appearing of the Lord. Temptation to sin is painful to us only as we are sanctified by the Spirit of grace, and walk with God.

We ought not to wish for deliverance from trial until the trial has done its office. Shall the gold be taken out of the furnace before the dross has been consumed?

Faith's expectation in the day of trouble is large showers of blessing.

Sorrow and temptation (1 Pet. 1:6-7) are the seeds of joy and praise. "They that sow in tears shall reap in joy" (Psalm 126:5).

Confidence in God proves itself in time of trial; it grows in the day of battle. David, in the valley of Elah, was most bold when the giant cursed him, and drew nigh to slay him.

God has blessed us with all spiritual blessings in heavenly places in Christ: we have oneness with Christ; we have faith and the Spirit: what more, then, do we need but the trial of faith and the Spirit's fellowship?

If we have a steadfast purpose to overcome temptation, sooner or later we surely prevail. Abraham, through the weakness of the flesh, did not leave his father when God commanded him to go into the land of Canaan; but it was his steadfast purpose to obey God; so that at the last, when he offered up Isaac, he conferred not with flesh and blood.

Are we content to leave our cause in the hands of God? Job should have done this at the first; but by justifying himself he increased his trouble.

James 1:2: "Count it all joy when ye fall into divers temptations." There is grace in Christ for our fulfilling the precept.

If, being tried, I am entangled in unbelief, I cannot count my trial joy; so to do, I must by the Spirit's power resist the Tempter.

Satan has no pity on us, be we sick or well: if he leave us for a season, it is because the time decreed is spent, and he cannot exceed his commission.

Faith never expects to learn *deep* lessons without *deep* difficulties; therefore she is not surprised by strange and dark providences.

How many are apt to say, "My temptation is peculiar!"[14] But we should remember that it is the peculiar aggravations which make a trial effectual, and should not forget the word, "There hath no temptation taken you, but such as is common to man" (1 Cor. 10:13).

Our faith is greatly strengthened when we are brought to see that no arm but God's can help; no wisdom but His can guide; and no love but His can satisfy.

The thickest cloud brings the heaviest shower of blessings.

Those very circumstances which make unbelief despond are meat and drink to faith.

14. unique

Satan is employed for God's people—for their discipline, their correction, their sifting, but not for their destruction.

Christ often wounds in order to heal; and if He give pain it is that we may find peace and rest in Himself. His wounds are full of kindness, and always tend to life, and health, and peace.

We often make this great mistake—we expect in the kingdom of patience what is only promised in the kingdom of glory; and we ask God rather for deliverance from the warfare than grace for it as long as He is pleased that it shall last. Our impatience for victory often increases the heat of the battle.

To preserve *purity of life* in time of temptation, we must take constant heed to *purity of thought*.

God has settled in heaven certain trials of our faith, which will as surely befall us as the crown of glory be given us at Christ's appearing. God's purposes of grace are a golden chain; not a link must be missing.

Temptations which find us dwelling in God are to our faith like winds that more firmly root the tree (James 1:2-4).[15]

How much of adversity do we need in order to bring down the lofty thoughts within us! A knowledge of our own weakness is generally learnt through humiliation and suffering.

Those trials which put our wisdom to confusion, thwart our pride, and starve the lusts of the flesh, best fit and enable us to trust the living God. Let us, then, not suffer such trials to pass without making right use of them, giving thanks to God for them all.

---

[15]. "My brethren, count it all joy when ye fall into divers temptations; knowing this, that the trying of your faith worketh patience. But let patience have her perfect work, that ye may be perfect and entire, wanting nothing."

He is most likely to fall into temptation and sin who most slights a warning. He who most truly depends upon the Lord for succour in the time of temptation will be the most thankful for counsel or reproof.

When a trial comes upon me, let me look upon it as sent for a peculiar blessing. If I receive it thus, I shall not consider "how heavy it is!" nor ask "when will it be removed?" but "how much advantage shall I gain through it? and how shall I turn it to the best account?"

Often when saints, by right steps, bring afflictions upon them, they are *tempted* to think their course wrong; but faith seizes the opportunity of glorifying God. Thus the *apparent* loss becomes great gain (Esther 4:13-16).

How much will our trials weigh when this mortal shall have put on immortality, and we shall appear with Christ in glory (2 Cor. 4:17-18)?

The troubles of the way do us good service, if they raise the eyes of our mind to look at things unseen and eternal.

Present faith, not past experience or comfort, keeps us from fainting in the hour of trial.

Which of us can be kept near to Christ without some thorn in the flesh?

Faith, patience, and prayer, can overcome all difficulties.

Affliction coming upon God's people is no proof that they are displeasing Him. Is God with them or not? is the test. Jeremiah was cast into the dungeon, and sank in the mire; but God was with him (Jer. 38). So was it with Joseph (Gen. 39:21).[16]

---

16. "But the Lord was with Joseph, and shewed him mercy, and gave him favour in the sight of the keeper of the prison."

We can never walk with steady step in the time of trial of our faith, save as we are looking onward to the resurrection of the just. In 1 Corinthians 15:58, the apostle, in view of it says, "Be ye steadfast, unmoveable, always abounding in the work of the Lord, forasmuch as ye know that your labour is not in vain in the Lord."

Difficulties and ill success encourage me; for "the life which I now live in the flesh, I live by the faith of the Son of God, who loved me, and gave Himself for me."[17]

Do we meet with unkindness from brethren? Instead of shooting our bitter words at them, let us *judge ourselves*; and endeavour, in love and wisdom, to overcome evil with good.

Is the child of God overwhelmed by the trials of the way, and ready to turn his back in the day of battle, because of the rage of hellish powers? Let me remind him that Samson first slew the lion, and afterwards out of the same lion got honey and to spare.

When God gave Paul the thorn in the flesh, he knew not at first the value of the gift, and would have cast it away, had he been left in his own hands. The Lord was his keeper, and taught him, and us by him, that the strength of Christ is made perfect in weakness.

---

17. Gal. 2:20

The Calling of the Church

The church is not only quickened by Christ, but quickened together with Him . . . . If this truth were received into the understanding and affections and lived upon daily by the children of God, their very garments would smell of myrrh and frankincense, with all powders of the merchant; and their conversation would bespeak their heavenly calling in Christ Jesus.

To rise above the first Adam we must live in the last Adam. We shall then be able in spirit to use the language of the 8th Psalm, and have all things under our feet.

Our life is in Christ: therefore it is *eternal life*; for Christ is "the same yesterday, today, and forever."

God's design was not only to save us from hell, however great that salvation, but to make us His sons and daughters, in order that we, with Himself and the Lord Jesus, the firstborn from the dead, might dwell forever in our Father's house.

True love has its source in Christ Himself. It is therefore bold in defence of His truth, and knows no man after the flesh when His honour is to be maintained or defended.

We have three chief characters to sustain—child of God; soldier; spouse of Christ. We have to feast; to fight; and to sing. Christ has won the victory. We gather up the spoils; and though so doing we must fight, the victory is ours and its fruit.

To have the Lord Jesus *revealed to us* by the Spirit of God is enough. It sufficed Stephen amidst his persecutors, and suffices us amidst all our difficulties and adversaries, amidst all trials, great and small.

God's people are His witnesses; they are the light in this dark world: they should therefore be so filled with the Spirit, as to be Christ's epistles, known and read of all men.

The church has spiritual, heavenly, eternal life in Christ, her risen Lord, the last Adam. His pierced side is the fountain of life to us His *spouse*.

We are under the law of God's love and grace in our new relation as *children*; we are under obligation to Christ as firstborn among many *brethren*; and as His *members*, to obey Him as our *Head*.

We have often the words *members of Christ* upon our lips; would that they were always accompanied with reverence and love!

Colossians 2:14:[18] The forgiveness of God is like the God who grants it—everlasting, all-comprehensive, immeasurable . . . . No possibility of condemnation. The bond that was against me is now nailed up, as it were, in the court of justice for the protection of the debtor. I now owe everything to the love of God; I owe my whole self. Let Christ dwell in my heart, to guide every glance of the eye, every thought of the mind.

How strange would it seem to us to see a prince in sorry garments seated on the ale-bench in company with common men! How much greater the inconsistency when a child of the living God, a king and a priest unto God, degrades himself to fellowship with the unregenerate!

In order of time we were in the first man Adam, the man of the earth, first: but not so in order of purpose and decree;

---

18. "Blotting out the handwriting of ordinances that was against us, which was contrary to us, and took it out of the way, nailing it to his cross . . . "

according to this we were in the last Adam, the second man, the Lord from heaven, ere we fell in the first.

Every flock bears the mark of its owner; so the sheep of Christ have their mark, even poverty of spirit; each one is a poor needy sinner, self-judged and self-condemned, according to the justice of God.

For a child of God to talk of his heavenly calling, and not to walk according to it, how sad a sight! The moment I am born of God, I am in the world in a new relation; I am a crucified man: and that I am such should be evident to all around.

God holds us accountable for what we have, and not for what we have not. If I have only ten minutes to read the Word, do I employ those ten minutes according to my accountability?

Many believers, though they live in New Testament times, walk in the Old Testament spirit.

The "New Creature"

The believer in Jesus, being created anew, has the likeness of God stamped upon him. In nature the child resembles the parent. There is no feature of the countenance of God the Father but is to be found in the feeblest child of grace (2 Pet. 1:4).[19]

According to the new man, we crave the knowledge of God's truth for the sake of obedience; but the flesh desires knowledge for the vain-glorious talk of the lips that tendeth to penury (Prov. 14:23).

As a vessel takes its shape from the mould, so should our will be formed in the mould of the will of God: then shall we have everything our own way (John 15:7).[20]

Christ had no will but the will of His Father, and in His delight to do that will we see His perfect holiness: for what is holiness but "Thy will be done"?

As the weakness of the old man lies in its vain conceit of its strength; so the strength of the new man lies in its true sense of perfect weakness.

God is no respecter of persons; but He will honour them that honour Him, whereas they that despise Him shall be lightly esteemed (1 Sam. 2:30). He honours us for His own grace in us, and corrects us for our evil ways.

---

19. "Whereby are given unto us exceeding great and precious promises: that by these ye might be partakers of the divine nature, having escaped the corruption that is in the world through lust."
20. "If ye abide in me, and my words abide in you, ye shall ask what ye will, and it shall be done unto you."

Unbelief

Unbelief is oft a hypocrite clothed in a white robe, as an angel of light, having the semblance of all humility; but drag him to the light, and the monster appears! He would cast down God from His throne and set himself thereon.

Where unbelief is, there is pride; and where pride is, her whole brood of evils are to be found with her. So with the obedience of faith, there is humility with all her train.

There will be no room for the fretfulness of unbelief, if I only see that He who is the Ruler of heaven and earth is my very Kinsman—my Brother.

When a child of God takes an unbelieving step, and God suffers it to succeed, this is one of the sharpest corrections he can be visited with (2 Chron. 16:2-9).

Let us not nourish unbelief by plans and contrivances of fleshly prudence.

One step of unbelief unrepented of leads to another.

Hard thoughts of God are, alas! natural to us; and swarm in our breast: it is only as the love of God is revealed to us in the cross of Christ that we are able to cast them out.

If in great tribulation we are by faith walking upon the flood, we shall seem to the eye of unbelief to be sinking in the flood.

If unbelief prevail in saints, they slight the assemblies of God's people; but let us who diligently frequent them be able to say, "We have seen the Lord" (John 20:25): that will be the best rebuke for the negligent.

Unbelief is in man's sight no sin at all—whilst in God's sight it is of all sins the greatest.

Whilst we are looking to Jesus at the right hand of God, all circumstances are our occasions for honouring God by faith; but if we look to circumstances and not to Christ, they cast us down, and leave us a prey to unbelief.

By unbelief the child of God degrades himself; losing sight of his heavenly robe he makes much of the earthly rags of this world's honour, and can even envy the wearers (Psalm 73:3).[21]

We do well to remember that God is as true to His forewarnings of wrath and curse, as He is to His promises of grace. We take the latter for our peculiar comfort, but should also solemnly meditate the former for our ripe and full acquaintance with God.

Unbelief cripples and puts in fear where no fear is; it leads to despair, and despair is but unbelief without a bridle.

Do you, at the Mercy-seat, confess the iniquity of unbelief? Remember that it makes God to be the very contrary of what He is.

Unbelief and its rebellion will make of a mere nothing a great mountain.

Every murmuring thought is the child of unbelief, and makes God a liar.

---

21. "For I was envious at the foolish, when I saw the prosperity of the wicked."

The Sins of Believers

The heart of man is a restless deep, ever casting up mire and dirt (Isa. 57:20); but in the sins of God's children there is a preeminence of guilt.

Jonah could not sin himself out of the love of God; therefore, sinning himself out of communion with God, he had the greater guilt.

I count myself more vile than the murderer who suffers death by the hangman's hand, because the atoning blood of the Son of God acquaints me with myself . . . . That which shows me my forgiveness reveals to me my pollution.

By far the greater part of the sins of God's children are sins of ignorance. How needful therefore the cry, "Cleanse Thou me from secret faults" (Psalm 19:12)—faults hidden from mine own eye and from mine own conscience. Without atoning blood they would bring down God's curse on the offender's head. Oh, let us not make light of sins of ignorance!

The sins of our unregenerate state should indeed be ever before us; but by frowardness, since we tasted that God is gracious, we sin (as natural men cannot sin) against the heart of Christ, against God's love and His Spirit, who seals us unto the day of redemption. The natural man is a rebel against his Maker; but it is against a Father that we, the saved, offend. Forgetting the cross, we go astray. The remedy is true and speedy confession; for we have an Advocate with the Father (1 John 2:1).[22]

---

22. "My little children, these things write I unto you, that ye sin not. And if any man sin, we have an advocate with the Father, Jesus Christ the righteous."

We must be ever waging war with the secret workings of sin. Where it is but in a little measure allowed, God may suffer His child to go further and further in that allowance, until the seven locks are shorn on Delilah's lap.

To be doubting Christ's love, to be limiting His grace, is alike unworthy of us and grieving to Him. The last offence of Joseph's brethren (Gen. 50:15-21) was not the least.

There is no fault in our character that the grace of God cannot cure. It becomes us therefore to give no quarter to the Canaanites (Judges 2).

God deals with us after conversion otherwise than before it: He, as a wise Father, has a rod of correction for His children, and smites them when He might let them alone, did they not know His love.

Peculiar temptations bring forth peculiar corruptions, after neglected warnings.

The Lord Jesus took loving pains to make Peter acquainted with Himself, and was compelled to humble him by his threefold denial of his Lord, but without exposing him to the eye of enemies. Overcome by a sudden temptation, he was quickly forgiven and restored (Luke 22:55-62). Whereas David, who had deliberately transgressed, and who had long been in a backsliding state of heart, was exposed to the people as well as made loathsome in his own eyes. (2 Sam. 12, 16). When Christ restores a fallen one, He often makes that disciple stronger than before his fall. "When thou art converted, strengthen thy brethren" (Luke 22:32). So it will be with those who, like David and Peter, have been wont to follow the Lord fully.

The people of God are in general slack and slothful in searching out sins of ignorance; but if we persevere in the search, asking

God to reveal them to us, He will give us very humbling knowledge of ourselves and of our secret faults; with it also blessed comfort and communion, which otherwise we could not enjoy.

The Coming of the Lord

Let the blessed hope of the coming of Christ keep us ever on the watchtower; looking, longing for it, and hasting towards it.

Would that we duly considered our accountability to Christ, who in the day of His appearing will judge the secrets of all hearts. Then we shall each be called on to give an account of his stewardship—an account, not only of gifts of understanding and substance, but of daily employment, and of all the minutes of the day. (See 1 Cor. 4:1-6.)[23]

---

[23]. "Let a man so account of us, as of the ministers of Christ, and stewards of the mysteries of God. Moreover it is required in stewards, that a man be found faithful. But with me it is a very small thing that I should be judged of you, or of man's judgment: yea, I judge not mine own self. For I know nothing by myself; yet am I not hereby justified: but he that judgeth me is the Lord. Therefore judge nothing before the time, until the Lord come, who both will bring to light the hidden things of darkness, and will make manifest the counsels of the hearts: and then shall every man have praise of God. And these things, brethren, I have in a figure transferred to myself and to Apollos for your sakes; that ye might learn in us not to think of men above that which is written, that no one of you be puffed up for one against another."

Prayer

It is a high place that is given to the prayers of saints in 1 Tim. 2:1-2.[24] If Christians only knew how their prayers for kings and governors are heard in heaven, they would not be meddlers with this world's politics.

Every wish that the Holy Ghost breathes into the soul of a believer is a voice which enters into the ear of God.

It is well for a child of God to pray for himself, but a more excellent thing to pray for others. God honours the spirit of intercession.

We are too apt to set God a time and a way of answering our prayers; and even when our prayers are answered, we are often surprised and ready to faint. If we desire much communion with God and with Christ, we must not be surprised if the Holy Spirit come upon us as a keen north wind, revealing our own corruption and evil to us: when it comes, let us not say, How can we bear this? but rather be thankful for God's wise answer to prayer.

If we have not the spirit of supplication and thanksgiving, let us begin with the spirit of confession.

When we pray, let us be sure God is hearing us. If we ask help, kindness, favour, from a fellow man, it cheers us to observe *the kind attentive look*: let us by faith regard our unseen Saviour and Priest, and settle it in our hearts that our prayer is received;

---

24. "I exhort therefore, that, first of all, supplications, prayers, intercessions, and giving of thanks, be made for all men; for kings, and for all that are in authority; that we may lead a quiet and peaceable life in all godliness and honesty."

the answer will come in the best time. If we cannot comply with God's just demands to be singing and triumphing with Christ above, He will listen to His unbelieving, groaning children. He *bows down* His ear to hear their cry.

When the Word of God enters the conscience, men pour out their hearts indeed to the Lord.

Our need of prayer is as frequent as the moments of the day; and as we grow in spirituality of mind, our continual need will be felt by us more and more.

In order to have power with God in prayer, there must be an undivided heart; if we would come boldly to the throne of grace, we must come obediently.

Daniel made prayer and meditation of the Scriptures the chief business of his life; yet, if we consider the circumstances in which he was placed, we shall see that few ever had greater obstacles than he in the way of seeking God.

God gives, as a wise Father, prized benefits to His supplicating children.

When we ask for more communion with God, are we willing to part with all that hinders? Let us take heed that our ways agree with our words when we come to the Mercy-seat.

It is a great help to us when we see that our prayers and our labours are to be as the grain of wheat falling into the ground. If we look for death and burial first, we shall be able to go on in patience; and in due time shall assuredly reap an abundant harvest.

We ought to go to God with our matters as altogether His.

How great is our favour and power with God! for we are kings and priests unto God—His sons and daughters by adoption and grace. Let us take heed that we grieve not the Spirit who sealed us unto the day of redemption; and nothing will God deny us (John 15:7).[25]

The best testimony that Stephen bore was his last: not when he was preaching and working miracles, but when he pleaded for his persecutors; for then he most resembled the Lord Jesus in patience, forgiveness, and love.

When some peculiar pressure is upon you, be like Queen Esther, whose first request was the king's company. In each trial "seek first the kingdom of God and His righteousness,"[26] and all other things shall be added: your seeking first the removal of the trial shows that you need the continuance of it.

We must not look on that only as prayer to which our lips give utterance; the wish of the believing heart is counted prayer by God; it is the smoke of the incense which ascends in silence before Him.

If a path be overgrown with moss and briers, it is difficult to trace it; if well frequented, it is plainly seen. Our pathway to the fountain of Jesus' blood should be ever well trodden by our confessions.

Unbelief lightly esteems both our own prayers and those of others.

We can never draw nigh to God in believing prayer, but the answer will be more than we had grace to hope for. Expectation from God is a precious fruit of prayer.

A guilty conscience stops prayer, but a cleansed conscience makes prayer to flow.

We may often have the spirit of prayer without the comfort of prayer.

---

25. "If ye abide in me, and my words abide in you, ye shall ask what ye will, and it shall be done unto you."
26. Matt. 6:33

Conflict

When the corruptions of the flesh, like an armed host, invade the soul, they aim first at the capital city, which is Faith. Success there would ensure possession of the whole land.

It is ever Satan's aim to debase the heart and conscience of the children of God. Their heart should be filled with Christ; their conscience ruled by His word and ways. Satan would entice away the heart from Christ, and set up in the conscience a standard inferior to that of Christ's example. Oh that the saints were not ignorant of Satan's devices, but willing to pluck out the right eye, to cut off hand or foot, rather than give place at all to the adversary.

Let our affections be resting in Christ, and engrossed with Him; then will all saints be dear to us in Him, because they are one with Him, and we shall please Him concerning them. To prevent our attaining to this grace, or to spoil us of it, is the aim of the powers of darkness that war against us.

It is only as we have rest in Christ, only as we have peace through faith in His atoning blood, only as we have the purged conscience, with the heart's affections set upon Christ, that we have any strength to war against our spiritual enemies: it is whilst we are fighting against them, that strength is given equal to the need, and we experience the precious sympathy of the Captain of our salvation. "Put on the whole armour of God" (Eph. 6:10-19). David put away the armour of Saul, and went against Goliath with nothing save the weapons of weakness.

Service

God, in fitting any servant for special service, often subjects him to painful discipline of soul: the end of this training is the breaking down of self-confidence, so that when at last the servant goes forth to his work he says, "Who am I?" The flesh will not say, "Who am I?" But to this we must be brought ere God can put us to honourable use.

We are not the most useful when most wordy, but when most prayerful.

Though God marks that which is wrong in His servants, notwithstanding all their faithfulness, He never forgets that which is right in them, notwithstanding all their imperfections.

If we do not live *beyond* time, we are not fit to live *in* time.

We cannot bestow kindnesses upon the unconverted for Christ's sake without obtaining peculiar fellowship with God.

That man is miserable who is wrapped up in himself and cares not for others; such a man keeps happiness outside, and bolts the door against her.

The ways of Christ in the days of His flesh are the true pattern for His people.

It is a mark of steady progress in the ways of God when a servant of Christ, like his Master, makes no choice of service, seeking only to please his Lord.

If by walking before God we rise above the praise of men, we shall not be vexed or discouraged by their disapproval and blame.

He that is humble, and ever desiring to serve others, will surely find others desiring to serve him.

If we have but the heart to serve Christ, He will surely employ us; and if He have any special service for us, He will grant us special guidance (Acts 8:26).[27]

The conversion of sinners, the prosperity of saints—these are precious things, but not the object of the soul: that should be to please God. The moment a servant acts independently, he acts from himself, and out of character (John 21:3).[28]

In all you do be the servant of Christ, forgetting yourself—engrossed with Him.

We need readiness of heart, and skilfulness of hands, to serve the church of God aright.

---

27. "And the angel of the Lord spake unto Philip, saying, Arise, and go toward the south unto the way that goeth down from Jerusalem unto Gaza, which is desert."
28. "Simon Peter saith unto them, I go a fishing. They say unto him, We also go with thee. They went forth, and entered into a ship immediately; and that night they caught nothing."

Service to Christ

There is much that the Lord's true servants do which no human eye takes knowledge of. What they do they are to do as to the Lord, and to look for reward from Him; learning also to have fellowship with Christ in His sufferings and service.

It is our wisdom not to seek praise of men: if, in our intercourse with saints, rather than look after a good name, we seek to approve ourselves to God, a good name will surely follow us.

Look not at the quantity, but at the quality of your service, whatsoever that service may be. If it be preaching, preaching is not the first thing: the heart must first be kept; then two or three words spoken in the power of the Spirit may avail more than many a long discourse.

Forgiveness

Peter said to our Lord, "How oft shall my brother sin against me, and I forgive him, until seven times?" (Matt. 18:21-22). What warrant had Peter for saying, "How oft?" Had he been standing at the foot of Mount Sinai, he might have said, "How oft?" Standing in the covenant of grace, we say, "Seventy times seven."

If we be called to judge offending brethren, we should judge before the Mercy-seat. There we are self-judged, as oft offending and oft forgiven.

Those injuries are often hardest to forgive which are only known to the injured and the wrong-doer.

If others act with want of uprightness towards us, and we are irritated, it is a proof that we are then dealing rather with the creature than with God.

Those are the best fitted for the work of reproof who are severe against themselves, but gentle towards others; whilst such as are forward to reprove most need reproof themselves.

Poverty of Spirit

We must live as beggars upon the love of Christ; we are never safe from snares but as we are thus poor in spirit.

Christ was the only one who could, without a struggle, be content to be "a worm, and no man" (Psalm 22:6).

The self-exalted person as much degrades himself in God's sight, as he exalts himself in his own.

We sink into nothingness as we grow up into Christ.

To grow in poverty of spirit is truly to grow in grace: "Without Me ye can do nothing" (John 15:5).

If we be sitting at the feet of Jesus, all carnal boasting is excluded, we have His mind of wisdom in all things, and cannot behave ourselves unseemly.

No rest have we for the sole of our foot except in Christ; and whenever a poor needy one seeks Him, He deals by such an one as did Noah by the dove. Noah put forth his hand and took her in unto him into the ark.

If we upbraid ourselves, Christ justifies. If we be dumb in our own defence, He opens His mouth to plead our cause, and our wounded hearts He binds up.

If I be content to be nothing, I cannot take offence; and when I am *really* humble, and know myself a *worm*, I shall not complain if trampled on.

Pride nourishes the remembrance of injuries: humility forgets as well as forgives them.

Lot never drew near enough to God to know his own heart; it was Abraham, and not Lot, who said, I am but "dust and ashes" (Gen. 18:27).

Evil Passions

Oh, how unseemly in a Christian are murmurings, envying, and such like! If we look beneath the surface we shall find the root of these things to be unmortified pride, and a conscience not purged.

Pride never stoops but to take a higher flight.

The drunkard, the murderer, the idolater, cannot enter into the kingdom of heaven. The sins of such are counted great even by the natural conscience; but covetousness, who condemns it? Yet the man who thirsts for gold is alike with the murderer accursed from God.

Satan gets no more advantage over us than we allow him.

It is one of Satan's great aims to seduce the children of God and the servants of Christ into error; if he cannot do that, he will tempt them to keep back part of the truth, or to dwell upon any other part rather than Jesus Christ, and Him crucified.

The sum of man's excellency is "dust and ashes": nevertheless, Satan deludes men into thinking themselves something; he helps them to carnal self-amendment and self-improvement, and so makes them blind to their true state before God.

Self-Knowledge and Self-Judgment

True self-judgment shuts out the adversary.

The more we exercise ourselves in self-judgment, the more will the flesh in us be discerned *by ourselves*, and the less will it be seen *by others*.

In our exercise of self-judgment, we should keep our eye upon the Advocate with the Father, else we shall have a self-vexing conscience which profits not.

Self-examination is a solemn and profitable business: it should mainly consist in this, "My soul, believest thou? Lovest thou?" (Heb. 11:6; 3:12-13; John 13:34-35; Rom. 13:10; 1 Cor. 13).

The custom of self-judgment is among the best of spiritual habits.

"The Lord is a God of knowledge, and by Him actions are weighed" (1 Sam. 2:3). Because God tries the *heart*, therefore, in instances innumerable, God's judgment condemns where man may approve and praise.

The oftener we invite Him with whom we have to do to use the keen edge of "the sword of the Spirit" in our own consciences, the less will there be in us for Satan's fiery darts to fix upon.

If we better considered that "we have an Advocate with the Father" (1 John 2:1), we should not go far from the paths of the Lord and the presence of God. This Advocate speaks to the pity and love as well as to the holiness of the Father. It was the Advocate who said, "The spirit is willing, but the flesh is weak" (Matt. 26:41). He knows all our circumstances, and the power of temptation and trial. Let it be the *first* business of the conscience to think of this "Advocate with the Father"; then what child of God will be slow to make confession whenever it is due?

Each one of us has in himself some especially besetting evil—a weight to be laid aside (Heb. 12:1).

Let *me* ask the Lord to give me self-knowledge; for self-knowledge, though a painful, is a necessary thing, worth all the trouble of the search, and all the mortification it may cost me.

When Israel suffers defeat before Ai, it is time to do what should indeed have been done before: to search out the Achan in the camp. (See Joshua 7.)

When I see a brother overtaken in a fault, let me beware of my own besetments, and seek to restore him in the spirit of meekness.

Humility and Self-Abasement

Self-humiliation brings with it tenderness of spirit; and as we sink in our own esteem, the Lord fulfils in us that precious promise, "To this man will I look, even to him that is poor and of a contrite spirit, and trembleth at My word" (Isa. 66:2).

If we be self-loathed, we shall be willing, when brought low, to sink lower still (2 Sam. 15:25-26).[29]

He that is self-abased before God, and so carries himself humbly towards others, must obtain honour; but if any child of God exalt himself, sure as God is, shame will come of that self-exaltation.

Our reputation is the last thing we are willing to lose: we cleave to it even when, in point of justification and peace with God, we have counted our own righteousness filthy rags. Let the saints take heed to their walk before God and man; but this done, so that they have in all things a conscience void of offence, let them account their reputation God's jewel, not their own.

Knowledge often exceeds grace; but communion with God and poverty of Spirit go together: if the one decline, so will the other.

The low place is the safe place; and whatever the tribulation, it will surely bring its blessings, God being trusted.

---

29. "Now therefore, I pray thee, pardon my sin, and turn again with me, that I may worship the Lord. And Samuel said unto Saul, I will not return with thee: for thou hast rejected the word of the Lord, and the Lord hath rejected thee from being king over Israel."

Samson was never so strong as when, through his own folly brought low and put to shame, he said, "Strengthen me, I pray Thee, O God, only this once" (Judges 16:28).

We are wont to consider David's slaying Goliath a great deed of faith, and such it was; but more to be admired is David's dominion over himself that marked his course. His blemishes and sins were not his character.

Confidence in God and self-distrust are sure companions.

It is true humility and true holiness to judge ourselves dead and buried with Christ as children of the first Adam, whatever the flesh within us; and as children of God raised up together with Christ, and seated with Him, the last Adam, the head of the new creation. We thus discern, and subdue, and loathe the flesh, which, though crucified with Christ in the account of God and of faith, is ever struggling to regain lost dominion. Satan, taking occasion by the flesh, would cast us down in the spirit of our minds from our heavenly places. Resisting him in faith, we wage the war of Ephesians 6. Good soldiers of Christ will have the peace of God ruling in their hearts. They cannot but live in peace; for the God of love and peace is with them. Schism and division proclaim the victories and triumphs of Satan. Would God we were all by His Spirit awakened to consider these things! The day is at hand that will make us and our ways all manifest; and we ourselves shall then no more mistake the talk of the lips for the obedience of faith.

Circumstances

Our circumstances are what we make them. If they be not by faith kept under our feet, they will by unbelief become our masters.

Our song of praise can never be checked unless we rejoice in circumstances, and in things around us, more than in God Himself.

It is to our shame that we are easily wrought upon by shifting circumstances. How good for us that we have an unchangeable God to rest in!

The natural man is the slave of circumstances.

Never let me be compelled to say, I have driven my stakes so deep into the earth that I cannot pull them up; but rather let me so pitch my tent that in a moment I may strike it at the bidding of the Lord (Num. 9:15-23).

All things are working together for good to them that love God; albeit sometimes in the way of chastening and judgment.

If we honour God in the little matters of our daily life, He will prepare greater occasions for our faith, and so put honour on the obedience that was little known to any but Himself. Abraham had so dealt with God about all the daily little matters of tent and household, that when the great occasion comes (Gen. 22) the man of faith shines forth.

God orders our steps in our natural state (the guilt of our sins our own) to further us in His service after regeneration (Gal. 1:15).

It matters little what our circumstances, if in the spirit of our mind we be before God offering up spiritual sacrifices acceptable to Him by Jesus Christ. To faith all circumstances are opportunities of pleasing God and serving Christ.

That station of life is most desirable which has least in it to cumber the spirit, and to entice away the heart from Christ. Shall we not then rather desire to stoop with our Lord, than to rise with the men of the world? Every state in life has temptations; but these thicken upon us, and grow in seducing power, according to rise in earthly honour.

Howsoever we may deplore the sin of one that has injured us, we ought to be thankful for the occasion of showing the mind of Christ towards the wrong-doer.

If our hearts be set upon enjoying the light of our Father's countenance, we shall find that all circumstances, bitter as well as sweet, will afford us opportunity of bearing something, or doing something, for His sake.

My happiness in Christ will grow through every new circumstance, if I have no will but God's. God, by all circumstances, delights to make glad His obedient children (2 Thess. 3:16).[30]

If we judge not God's character by His providences, but His providences by His character, we shall be able to rejoice when the flesh would repine.

When Elijah in unbelief fled from Jezebel, he had the meet rebuke from the Lord; but the fault of the hour of temptation did not hide from God's gracious eye the faithfulness of His servant (1 Kings 19). In like manner dealt the Lord Jesus with that other Elijah—John the Baptist—when he seemed like a reed shaken

---

30. "Now the Lord of peace himself give you peace always by all means. The Lord be with you all."

with the wind (Matt. 11:2-15). We are to be imitators of God as dear, as pleasant, children; and if we are not to suffer sin upon our brethren, whatever their grace, neither should the fault in them be a cover to our eyes of their grace and service to Christ.

Strength and Continuance

Philippians 3:12: It is Christ's hold upon us that enables us, by faith, to lay hold on and to keep hold of Him.[31]

They who seem the most tried are not always those that have the sharpest warfare.

Sometimes things appear to us so difficult that we are daunted; at other times so easy that we think we are equal to them; and thus in either case we fail.

He that is running a race looks not at witnesses admiring, but only at the mark.

We need to "discern the Lord's body," i.e., Christ having been crucified (1 Cor. 11:29) for steadfastness of communion with God, no less than to trust in His blood to obtain salvation from wrath to come (John 6:54, 56).

The fulfilling of God's promises depends not upon the creature's strength, and cannot be prevented by the creature's weakness.

We need a close walk with God, a having respect to all His commandments, if we would obtain of Him whatsoever we ask.

True persevering diligence in spiritual things always begins in self-abasement.

It is one mark of growth in spirituality to be more afflicted by the pleasing—than by the distressing—temptations of Satan.

---

31. "Not as though I had already attained, either were already perfect: but I follow after, if that I may apprehend that for which also I am apprehended of Christ Jesus."

We should always take great trials and great temptations as the forerunners of great blessings and growth of fellowship with God.

The obedience of grace obtains for us the profitable knowledge of truth, and teaches us to prize it more than much fine gold. Mere knowledge puffeth up, and the talk of the lips tendeth only to penury (Prov. 14:23).

Deep spirituality of mind is only obtained by a thorough crucifixion of self: self-denial is discipline for life—the work of every hour.

To make a good soldier, put him in front of the battle; a good seaman, let him brave the storm: so with the Christian.

True readiness to confess sin, and joy in self-abasement, mark a growth in grace and knowledge of the character of God.

I know of no one who, with so little promise in his beginnings of faith, had a sunset so glorious as had Jacob (Gen. 48, 49).

It is the constant crucifying the flesh in little things that makes a giant in the Christian warfare. But true self-crucifixion is a thing impossible, save by grace; and to have the needful supplies of that grace we must be in perpetual communion with God: it is only thus we shall overcome in little things.

It is a great salvation wrought for us, if the soul be resolved to suffer the will of God, cost what it may.

Do you desire a humble mind, a soft heart, an obedient spirit? Ask and receive, that your joy may be full. But remember, "The soul of the sluggard desireth, and hath nothing" (Prov. 13:4). Be the clean vessel that God delights to fill and use.

Not God's answering prayer in respect of earthly things and earthly gifts, but growth of the new man, is the true proof that we please God.

We are commanded to lay aside every weight, and the sin that does so easily beset us: if we contend not against the latter—that is unbelief—how shall we rightly deal with the former? We have every one in himself his own peculiar hindrances—weights which, if not laid aside, will clog the soul in her race.

How shall I run my race and not stumble? How shall I have Christ's approval in the day of His appearing? are questions to be daily put by every child of God to his own soul.

Character

In the members of Christ, even those in whom much excellency of character is manifest, too often, alas! we find the "flies of death" in the apothecary's ointment (Eccles. 10:1); but in the Lord Jesus all excellences are blended in full perfection and harmony: He is the "altogether lovely" (Song of Sol. 5:16). But oh for a conversion of saints!—that we who are renewed, anointed, and sealed by the Spirit of God; that we in whom dwells that Holy Spirit of promise, who are the temple of God—might be altogether like our Lord, altogether pleasing to Him. Blessed be God, His people Israel must be by-and-by His delightsome child knowing and doing His will (Isa. 62).

Walking with God teaches us the courtesy and kindness of love.

We do not glorify God so much by what we do, as by what we are. It is the spirit of our mind which glorifies Him. "I dwell," says Jehovah, "in the high and holy place; with him also that is of a contrite and humble spirit" (Isa. 57:15).

If we walk much with God and with Christ, it will give us a certain *rightness of character*, so that we shall have the ready grace for every circumstance.

God with us makes our service honourable, be that service what it may.

Obedience

David was keeping sheep in the wilderness with no eye upon him but God's. In prompt obedience to his father he went to the valley of Elah, taking loaves and cheeses to his brethren: if we are content to serve God in mean things, God will bring us forth in greater. In the valley of Elah was Goliath ready for David's sling (1 Sam. 17:17-23).

Obedience to Christ brings upon us opposition from Satan, the world, the flesh in ourselves, and the unbelief, ignorance, and lack of mind of Christ in our brethren. To meet all these aright, let it be our business, even in the smallest matters, *to please Christ*, that we may have *His* power and *His* truth for our strength and guidance. He trod this path before us, and has also given His Holy Spirit to lead us and to comfort us through the journey.

The highest attainment in the spiritual life is to be able always and in all things to say, "Thy will be done!" Genesis 22 gives us a perfect sample of the obedience of faith.

There is no prevailing against our enemies without full obedience to God. When Israel must fight, Joshua must take heed that they are keeping God's commandments. (See Joshua 7.)

He that allows himself in small sins will at length break out in great ones: be it our business, then, to watch against the beginnings of departure from God, or these will surely lead to bitter endings.

The Word of the Lord, and the attentive ear of the faithful servant, are all we need to carry us safely and happily onward.

Whatever imperfections were in Abraham, whatever his haltings and stumblings, he never settled down, as to purpose, into half-hearted obedience; so if any child of God, howsoever he may fail, have a steady, fixed purpose to please God, he will surely become strong in faith at the last.

All the children of God receive Christ as Redeemer from curse and wrath; but they do not all take Him for their portion and inheritance: if we do this, we cannot fail to be witnesses for Him, and lights in this dark world.

Cares

Have you one anxious thought you do not bring to Jesus? Have you one care you deem too light, too small, to lay before Him? It is then too small to give you one moment's concern. Either cast your care (great or small) upon Him that careth for you, or cast it away from you altogether: if it be unfit for His sympathy, it is unworthy of you (1 Peter 5:7).[32]

If we examine the troubles of God's children, we shall find that too many of them arise from unbelieving fears concerning the future; let me but remember that Christ, at the right hand of God, counts *all my* troubles *His own*; and then away with all my fears concerning the morrow! It is only at the Mercy-seat we may lawfully think of the morrow.

---

32. "Casting all your care upon him; for he careth for you."

Chastisement

To quarrel with the instruments God used for our correction is to quarrel with God Himself. It is, in fact, to say to Him, "I do not approve of Thy government, and I could order matters better if they were left to me." What is this but to aim at casting down God from His throne, and setting ourselves thereon?

Though the Lord often spares reproof, He never spares commendation. He is slow to anger; He makes haste to be gracious (Neh. 9:17; Psalm 40:13).

Jacob underwent discipline and chastisement for upwards of fifty years, for the withering in him the evil root of the spirit of unbelieving contrivance. God blesses His child, and in His very love withholds not the rod of correction.

The pain that God's discipline gives us shows its wisdom: it is the diseased part that *feels* under the surgeon's hand.

God never puts us to shame before the world, or even before the church, unless we compel Him.

The Lord always deals with us according to the state of our souls.

How small the knowledge of God that Job would have attained to, but for the deep and marvelous discipline whereby he was sifted and taught!

When we deal with God in prayer about the difficulties of our path, we must not set Him a time for clearing away those difficulties, but wait upon Him, who accepts the sacrifice of our willing hearts.

The Lord's jewels need grinding, and cutting, and polishing. Why forget?

It is not of necessity that a child of God beginning well goes on well; but if he take good heed to his ways—according to Psalm 119, 2 Peter 1:5-7, and like Scriptures—he will surely run well to the end of his race.

The more bitter the cup of discipline, the more reason for our thankfulness. If we be not thankful, let us give God no rest, nor ourselves, until He make us so.

Correction despised brings sharper correction.

When God visits us with certain special discipline, it is our wisdom to accept the cup and drink it cheerfully, however bitter, for health is in it.

Let us have no reserves of conscience. When God gives us light, let us follow it whithersoever it may lead; for, while God has no judgments of curse for His children, He has judgments of displeasure of love because of disobedience.

Be more desirous of inward help and deliverance, than the removal of God's hand, when He lays affliction upon you.

Impatience under God's corrections only shows our need of the discipline He is pleased to visit us with. We can least bear correction when we most need it.

One of the evil fruits of long-continued spiritual negligence is the soul's ignorance of its own state.

How often, under discipline, are the children of God struggling amidst the thicket and briers of circumstances, instead of judging the state of their hearts! This lack of pondering their ways prevents their seeing the equity of God's dealings with them.

Discipline

Wherefore all the discipline with which Job was exercised? He could say in truth, "I know that my Redeemer liveth" (Job 19:25). As God's witness there was none like him in all the earth. He walked in uprightness, humility, patience, and wisdom; a perfect and upright man, fearing God and eschewing evil. Why then his afflictions and humiliations, before unheard-of among the saints? There was the flesh in Job; and the sifting discipline went on, until Job had learnt so to know both God and himself as to abhor himself and justify God.

I seek to keep short accounts with God: this saves not only much trouble and time, but also much sharp discipline.

"A reproof entereth more into a wise man than an hundred stripes into a fool" (Prov. 17:10).

It is indeed rare, when judgments come upon men, that those judgments yield their due profit. Those who walk with a tender spirit before God profit more by a word or gentle rebuke of His love, that none but themselves know of, than do others, who are careless walkers, by heavy judgments. If, however, great afflictions come, the heart being prepared, the end will be the double blessing (Job 42).

The cry of "Abba, Father!" in the time of trouble is often a sign of quick deliverance. When we kiss the hand that smites, the rod drops. Is it not to resist the will of God when we flee from those trials which He sends to prove our faith?

As children we may ask for understanding of our Father's will; but it belongs not to us to think for Him.

We may be sorrowful, yet not unhappy. Unhappiness is caused by self-will that frets against the Lord's way of dealing with us. But we may have sorrow without sinning, and by such sadness the heart is made better (Eccl. 7:3). Grace does not steel the heart, but makes it more tender. We may feel, but must not rebel.

Every child of God needs to be put into the sieve: but when sifted, if we be willing to endure the Lord's dealings with us, we shall not be put to shame.

How *few* the words of Jesus when all the earth, in its representatives—Herod, Pilate, priests and elders—rose up against Him! He never uttered more or less than was needed for God's glory. That perfect guidance of the tongue proceeded from the perfect subjection of His will to God.

The proper fruit of the Lord's discipline is that blessed state described by the psalmist, when the fretting of the flesh is silenced, the soul composing itself to rest in the everlasting arms. "Surely I have behaved and quieted myself, as a child that is weaned of his mother: my soul is even as a weaned child" (Psalm 131:2).

It is not every child of God who, by reason of acquaintance with God and with himself, reckons upon discipline, and resolves to go through it with God, how bitter soever it may be: hence when it comes he frets; he is the bullock unaccustomed to the yoke (Jer. 31:18).

Christ had a lawful desire to be spared suffering. He could not otherwise have been a pattern to us of patience and submission: but *His* submission brought Him into the floods of His sufferings. *Our* afflictions are light, soon as we can say, "Not my will, but Thine be done."

Deep inwrought patience is precious fruit of suffering God's will according to God's mind.

If we desire that patience have her perfect work, we shall thank the only-wise God for all things whatsoever that afflict us; and whosoever they be that God uses for pruning our souls—be they unjust men or froward brethren—we shall love and pray for them, and seek to overcome their evil with good.

A child of God may be greatly afflicted, yet be far from murmuring against his heavenly Father. Sorrow sanctified obtains God's embrace; rebellious grief spoils the soul of communion. The cluster must be bruised to yield its wine, and the sufferings of heavenly patience procure for the soul an overflowing cup of consolation, both for its own comfort and that of others (2 Cor. 1:4-6).

How many snares, how much harm, and loss, and shame, would the people of God avoid and escape, had they a little more patience in waiting for the Lord! Had Saul but waited a few minutes longer for Samuel then "would the Lord have established his kingdom upon Israel for ever" (1 Sam. 13:13).

Experience

It is only as by faith we see our Home above, that we are proper pilgrims here.

We rightly use our past experience, if, in time present, we have no confidence in the flesh.

Experience obtained without much waiting on God is not worthy the name: "Patience worketh experience" (Rom. 5:4).

Our past experience should be well pondered before God. The record of the pilgrimage of every one of us will be found in the great book of God's government, by-and-by to be opened.

God requires steadfastness of faith from those who have had especial proofs of His love.

The spring of instability of purpose is some hankering within us after praise of man.

The more we walk with God, the more we shall sorrow for our sins and those of others. This sorrow well consists with joy in the Holy Ghost.

We never hinder another's service or grace without hindering our own: "Quench not the Spirit."

Let us always be aiming at perfection: thus we shall grow in the knowledge of our imperfection.

"Tribulation worketh patience"; but if tribulation pass by without working patience, we cannot have "experience" (Rom. 5:3).

A Sound Mind

One special mark of a sound mind is a readiness to take counsel of God, and a bringing into subjection all notions of our own or of others to His revealed will.

It is not by change of circumstances that we can be made happy, but by submission to the will of God. This submission is manifested by our steadfast purpose to mortify the will of the flesh, and by our contending against everything that offends God.

Without confidence in the love of God we cannot cheerfully submit to His discipline.

Let not the morrow be as a thief to rob you of this day's blessing.

We are apt to judge of things by present appearances; but the Lord sees them in all their consequences.

Murmurers always extol times past as better than the present. The people of Israel in Egypt groaned by reason of hard bondage. Having passed the Red Sea, they sang the song of redemption: but how ready were they to say one to another, "Let us make a captain, and let us return into Egypt" (Num. 14:4). Had Moses desired to shame them, he might have asked: "What said you under Pharaoh's yoke?"

Danger and Temptations

If we would keep the creature in its place, we must take God as our portion.

Being an heir of glory, I would, by God's grace, rather break stones on the road for Him than be put to the drudgery of ruling an empire.

Spiritual prosperity is always attended with strong temptation to the *high thought*, the *lofty imagination*.

The worst temptations are those which so pamper and please the flesh that they do not vex us at all: they are perilous by their deceitfulness.

The outward falls of the children of God always bespeak the foregoing state of the heart.

The wearing of apparel is a special mark of our fall and shame. How unseemly then is pride of dress! Does the convict glory in the convict's coat?

The Christian's Walk

If we can fight well in the closet, we shall walk happily with God in all His ways. We should begin our every day's journey with *Him*: and, comparing need with supply, shall we not take pleasure in infirmities and necessities? because Christ will thereby take occasion to magnify His grace, and to lead us to springs of consolation in Himself.

Evil speaking has place in the heart before it escapes the lip.

Happy they who never hang upon the creature's favour: they who expect everything from God and nothing from man will have no disappointment.

To be a true witness for Jesus I must be much in His company, hear His voice, and observe His ways. How can we know the character of one with whom we have but little intercourse?

Humility helps us to know our pride; and if we would have the "rest" that is for the lowly, we must tread under foot our pride (Matt. 11:29).

Those temptations which prove the most defiling are ofttimes the least painful.

When God's will rules in us, and overrules our will, we shall then indeed, but not till then, know the pleasures of *having our will* (1 John 3:22; 5:14-15).[33]

---

33. "And whatsoever we ask, we receive of him, because we keep his commandments, and do those things that are pleasing in his sight . . . . And this is the confidence that we have in him, that, if we ask any thing according to his will, he heareth us: And if we know that he hear us, whatsoever we ask, we know that we have the petitions that we desired of him."

The Christian's path in the world is obedience to Christ; following Him, suffering for His sake. When we take part with the world to put it in order, and to make the crooked straight, we, as it were, take off our robes of heavenly priesthood to act as citizens of earth.

We ought so to walk before the world, that the evil eye, looking for a blot, may find none. The people of the world are keen judges of what a child of God should be.

Did the children of God walk worthy of God, they would no more seek worldly honours and glories than a king's son in his princely apparel would stitch thereon a beggar's rags.

"Bless them that curse you" (Matt. 5:44). The deed of grace is to be done at the moment of receiving the injury. When the curse proceeds from the mouth of the enemy, let the blessing proceed from yours. Remember the words, "Father, forgive them," "Lord, lay not this sin to their charge" (Luke 23:34; Acts 7:60).

There is light for the pilgrim's path, though there be not an unclouded sky.

If a man's heart were filled with Christ and His coming in glory, would it not be seen in all his ways—whether in the family, the church, or the world?

To be spiritually-minded is "life and peace" to ourselves: but how profitable to others also! That utterance and knowledge may be used aright, he that has them must walk with God.

Let Christ be with you wherever you go, and let it be known that His presence is with you.

Take good heed to your walk: God will care for your good name.

God has great ends to answer by leaving His children in the world; even that they may be living witnesses for Him whom they love—the unseen Lord Jesus. We should be ever giving thanks for such an office; and for our continuance on earth, that we may fulfil it.

Let us be pilgrims, not by constraint, but by loving choice.

Trial of the Servants of Christ

When Christ would put peculiar honour upon His servants, He often suffers them to be brought low in the sight of men. If the saints are favoured to suffer reproach for Christ's sake, then will they own the honour put upon them to be thus conformed to their Master. Paul and Silas, thrust into prison at Philippi, sang praises to God.

Christ never allows any faithful servant of His to suffer loss, but He turns that loss to great gain.

God always honours faithful servants, and comforts persecuted ones.

Dealing with the Faults of Others

If we would wisely reprove the flesh in our brethren, we must first, after the Lord's example, remember and commend the grace in them.

Those who are much acquainted with the cross of Christ, and with their own hearts, will be slow to take the reprover's office: if they do reprove, they will make it a solemn matter, knowing how much evil comes of the unwise handling of a fault.

Let us begin by searching ourselves, if we would be profitable reprovers of others.

Much self-judgment makes a man slow to judge others; and the very gentleness of such an one gives a keen edge to his rebukes.

In reproving sin in others, we should remember the ways of the Holy Spirit of God towards us. He comes as the Spirit of Love; and whatever His rebukes, He wins the heart by mercy and forgiveness through Christ.

To forgive without upbraiding, even by manner or look, is a high exercise of grace—it is imitation of Christ.

If I have been injured by another, let me bethink myself—How much better to be the sufferer than the wrongdoer!

The flesh would punish to prevent a repetition of wrongs; but grace teaches us to defend ourselves without weapons. The man who "seventy times seven" forgives injuries is he who best knows how to protect himself.

If one do me a wrong, let me with the bowels of Christ seek after him, and entreat God to move him to repentance.

We partake in the guilt of an offending member of Christ, until we have confessed his sin as our own (Dan. 9), mourned over it, prayed for its forgiveness, and sought in the spirit of love the restoration of the erring one.

If our tongue have been betrayed into speaking contemptuously or even slightingly of an absent brother, let us quickly say, Alas! we have wounded Christ.

If in love I speak to a brother of his fault, it is because I hate the sin. If I speak of it with backbiting tongue, it is self-pleasing that moves me.

If under the law, when the bond was only in the flesh, the Israelite must not suffer sin upon his brother (Lev. 19:17), how much less should it be suffered under the gospel, which binds the saints together spiritually and eternally!

The figure of the mote in the eye shows what skill and tenderness he has need of who would be a reprover to his brother. Who would trust so precious a member as the eye to a rough, unskillful hand?

The Lord loves to manifest peculiar tenderness towards those who have been brought low, even though it may have been through their own folly. "Go tell His disciples . . . *and Peter*" (Mark 16:7).

Evil Speaking

We shall not escape the tongues of others, unless we first escape from self-love and self-flattery.

No sword so sharp as the tongue.

Only the bridling of the heart can effectually bridle the lips.

The backbiter is one who maliciously speaks evil of others; the babbler does so through lack of the thoughtfulness of love.

Deep and Silent Work

What is most precious in the sight of God is often least noticed by men.

The work of the Holy Ghost is often most mighty when least of its power is seen by the common eye. Judas working miracles, and King Saul prophesying, were not such proofs of the Spirit's power as the tears of Peter after he had denied his Lord.

If we would be strong, we must make pleasing God our business: then what adversary can harm us?

Before our knowledge can be of much profit to others it must become a channel of our own soul's communion with God in secret.

How needful is it to take heed to our ways, to seek counsel, not only of God, but of those who are faithful and prudent! Satan watches for our halting, and entangles us by little and little; questionable things first, then things plainly evil. Great sins may spring out of little trespasses.

That confession to others which is frequent and unasked is seldom deep before God.

They are most alive to snares and temptations who by reason of walking with God are most blameless: we rarely see the snare when entangled therein.

David, Elijah, and others, obtained victories over themselves in solitude, and there had power with God: when afterwards they came forth, how calmly did they undertake the greatest things, and how easily perform them!

How great a victory was that which Jonathan must have gained over himself, when he rejoiced to see David raised above him! He discerned the mind of God in David, and had so learnt to delight in God, that he did not see in David one who was to outshine him, but another faithful man raised up for God and for Israel. Not so Joab, who in hellish jealousy slew his kinsman Amasa (1 Sam. 23:17; 2 Sam. 20:9-10).

To *have* nothing, and to *be* nothing, this is riches, quietness, rest.

Little Things

Who would have thought that from Pharaoh's daughter going to bathe in the river of Egypt would spring the deliverance of Israel?

The mind of Christ in us is chiefly to be seen in *little things*. To walk before God in the everyday matters of life, and to have our words and actions savoured daily with the name of Jesus, this is true holiness.

In the least matters what need there is of looking upwards! I ought not to write a note without looking up to God, seeking His help; for I can write folly enough in one sentence to cause myself and others disquietude for months.

Let us turn every circumstance of the day into an occasion of communion with God. Things of small amount will then bring us great blessings.

In small points of obedience are found the best test of the soul's state.

What great grace it needs to find no excuses for our little faults!—still greater to confess them!

Fruit

God sometimes sends us a wintry season that we may the better bring forth summer fruit.

It is the way of the Lord to work for a season, as it were, underground: and as the seed that dies in the earth, through dying, comes to life, so God will seem to cut off the hope of fruit of our labour; yet when we have humbled ourselves under His hand, and He has secured the glory to Himself, He will put forth His power and bring to life our buried hopes.

There may be much communion with God when there is but little comfort in the soul, and much fruitfulness when there is but little joy and gladness. We bear fruit when we credit the Word of God against appearances, and when we submit our will to His.

There is no security for our bringing forth fruit in time to come, if we are not bringing forth fruit in the present hour.

How often we fail and miscarry toward the end of a trial of patience!

Do not expect to make great strides at once in believing; or that deep sanctification is to be wrought in a day.

We can never be said to have outlived our usefulness, unless we have outlived our spirituality.

We must first come to the withering of the flesh, before we can become spiritually strong and fruitful.

Christian Communion

We need one another; are dependent on one another—not as *fountains*, but as *channels* of blessing.

When mutual intercession takes the place of mutual accusation, then will the differences and difficulties of brethren be overcome (Job 42:8, 10).[34]

The infirmities of our brethren are fair occasions for our patience and long-suffering: let us have grace for each opportunity.

The hearts of true believers crave a fellowship which will last—a fellowship in the Spirit with each other, because of common fellowship with the Father, and with His Son Jesus Christ.

Humility is the secret of fellowship, and pride the secret of division.

If Christ be not the bond of friendship and of communion, and if His blood be not the life of love, how quickly may indifference take the place of warm affections, and how easily may close friends turn to stubborn adversaries, through the clashings of self-seeking and thwarted pride, or man's native fickleness!

In John 17 and in Ephesians 1, we see what the Church is in the sight of God in Christ—what it ought to be in its ways; and

---

34. "Therefore take unto you now seven bullocks and seven rams, and go to my servant Job, and offer up for yourselves a burnt offering; and my servant Job shall pray for you: for him will I accept: lest I deal with you after your folly, in that ye have not spoken of me the thing which is right, like my servant Job . . . . And the Lord turned the captivity of Job, when he prayed for his friends: also the Lord gave Job twice as much as he had before."

would be, did we not grieve the Holy Ghost, which is given to us to lead us into all truth, and to glorify Christ in us. But the Church has not been true to her heavenly calling; she has forgotten her dignity; she has lost her strength; the grey hairs are here and there upon her, and she knoweth it not (Hosea 7:9).

The fellowship of believers ought to be like the fellowship of the Father and the Son: any differences of judgment, therefore, which arise between two members of Christ about the truth of God should be a cause of humiliation, but not of strife and separation. God would soon make His children of one mind, did they steadfastly set their faces toward the Mercy-seat, seeking unity according to 1 Corinthians 1 and Ephesians 4-5.

It is sweet to talk of Jesus with our brethren, the children of God: but how much sweeter is it to talk with the Lord Jesus Himself!

If there be but a shadow of disunion between us and any brother or sister, let us not give ourselves rest until we bring about a reconciliation; let us search out what in our own ways may have caused the breach, and seek after a communion with our brother like that of the Father with His dear Son. We should, moreover, watch against everything in us that may wound or grieve our brother, so that we may be wise to prevent breaches of fellowship; observant of 1 Corinthians 13; our ways fashioned by the love that behaves itself not unseemly, and which faileth not. Nor shall we be skillful to heal breaches, if we be not watchful to prevent them.

The secret of lasting fellowship is that Christ is the life of it. He maintains, rules, and sanctifies its mutual tender love and confidence, which will grow more heavenly the more we are like Christ, the more we abide in Him. When He comes in His glory, what joy will it be to remember former friendships and see Jesus Himself, the spring and the stability of them all!

Suppose all the saints in a town met together in one place, with no outward sign of division; yet, if it were not the common aim to be of one mind with God, and with Christ, the Spirit would still be grieved by divisions of heart and judgment.

The communion of the members of Christ with each other is by the Holy Ghost, who, dwelling in them, gives them fellowship with the Father and with the Son. The oneness of mind between the Father, the Word, and the Holy Ghost, is the spring and pattern of the one new mind that should be found in, and mark out, the members of Christ.

Unless we have a spiritual understanding of this divine unity, we cannot rightly grieve for the divisions of God's people. By looking into this glass, we discover the nature and the guilt of schisms and divisions.

Love

"God is love" (1 John 4:16). His children please Him only so far as they are like Him, and "walk in love" (Eph. 5:2).

True heavenly love has its life and root in the cross of Christ; it has the single eye, and is its own recompense; endures ingratitude, and survives indifference and contempt; has quick sense of wrongs, but is ready to forgive; and covers a multitude of sins. The love we speak of is meek and lowly; behaves itself wisely and edifies; bearing with the foolish and self-conceited, while it shuns their folly. This holy love is the durable work of the Spirit of God: it proves faithful in wintry days; and, ever ready to "rejoice with them that do rejoice," adds gladness to their days of sunshine.

If we would so love all saints as to please God, we must bear in mind that their names are written in heaven and on Christ's heart; otherwise we shall love some because they are lovely, and dislike others because of their blemishes.

We only know the heart and thoughts of others by proof of word or deed. If a brother wound us, we should first hear him, and hear him thoroughly, before we judge him to be in fault; but in many cases we may find ourselves not less to blame than our brother.

The "more excellent way" is love, which beareth all things, hopeth all things, imputeth no evil. Nevertheless, if love see a fault, love will reprove in faithfulness the fault it *sees*. I say *sees*, for love is discerning, and love is faithful. I cannot but deal in such faithfulness with all my brethren, and entreat them to smite me in like manner, which, indeed, is to anoint my head with "excellent oil" (Psalm 141:5).

If we delight in God's glory, we shall delight to honour those whom God honours, and shall ourselves be no losers thereby.

Justice and Judgment

Every man stands before God on the ground of justice. The unregenerate sinner stands in his own name, and obtains death, "the wages of sin": the believing sinner stands in the name of Jesus; and because sin was borne by the Lord Jesus, and justice satisfied, has everlasting life.

As deeds and thoughts of wicked men do now appear to the all-seeing eye of God, so will He represent them to their memory and conscience at the great day: the offender will be chief witness against himself.

The children of God enter heaven, not by sufferance, but by right and title: the justice of God demands it, because Christ has died and is risen.

The justice of God can never show mercy where sin is imputed. No mercy, therefore, was shown to Christ. As the sinner's surety He drank the cup of vengeance to the dregs; and now the cup He gives us overflows with blessings.

Christ never keeps a man outside who knocks at His door; but those who will not come as beggars, who are blinded by pride, self-will, and unbelief—how can they complain if sent empty away?

The Love of God

We speak of Christ showing His love by the death of the cross; let us also evermore consider the Father's love, in whose hand was the sword. Oh, the yearnings of His heart, when He was bruising the Son of His love!

The children of God ought to count it their chief joy, in drawing nigh to God, that they have His ear and heart. Great is the difference between a child of God confiding in Him, and a child of God full of petitions and burdens, but doubting God until some outward deliverance be granted. The character of God and His love demand our perfect trust at all times.

The love of God is not purchased for us by the blood of Christ. That love springs up out of God's own heart and nature. Self-moved, He sent His Son.

We could not be the object of the Father's love, which is from everlasting to everlasting, but as chosen in Christ. He loves us with love perfect and unchangeable.

The Heart and Its Deceitfulness

David would never have fallen into gross outward sin, had he not been too familiar with it in his heart; there had the evil been ofttimes committed before it broke out in the wicked deed. Nor would he have numbered the people, had he not first strayed from the presence of God, and so become puffed up with pride (2 Sam. 11; 1 Chron. 21).

Saints rarely see the guilt of a murmuring, unbelieving spirit, while they do feel the discomfort and weakness it brings with it. How great the deceitfulness of sin that can hide such guilt from the conscience of a child of God.

The Lord would have us all deal truly with our state, and with our hearts. We cannot otherwise deal truly with Him.

When we desire any special guidance, let us look first at the state of our heart: we have natural reason; let us take heed that we put it not into the hands of the devil by self-will, but into the hands of God.

The mistake of ignorance is one thing; the darkness of self-will is another. There may be the former though the eye be single, but not the latter.

It is good for a child of God to search his heart, that he may know whether it is by nature or by grace that he is kept from outward evil. Fear of shame, love of reputation, power of conscience, natural affection, self-interest, greatly preserve the unregenerate from the commission of sin; and may in part also keep the children of God from defiling their garments; but it is only by the power of grace, and when the heart keeps the life, that our "good conversation" is a sweet savour to God.

The great outlet of sin is the tongue; the great inlets of temptation are the ear and eye; but of the whole body the heart is mistress. Therefore let grace rule the heart, and the whole man shall be subject.

The Form of Godliness

The enmity of the carnal mind is wont to hide itself by imitating the outward forms of the kingdom of God. The grace of God subduing the heart to Christ is the sign of the birth from above.

The drunkard and the thief are evidently in the broad road that leadeth to destruction. The Pharisee seems to tread the narrow way, yet does but keep the clean side of the broad road.

All who build their hope of eternal life on their prayers, reading the Scriptures, and other outward works of righteousness come short of the rest that is in Christ and the salvation that is in Him. The sinner's hands must be emptied of all such recommendations: it is with his poverty, and his poverty only, that he must come to the crucified Son of God.

The sinner that comes with his own good works to God for eternal life is a debtor who brings a bag of base coin of his own forging to pay his creditor withal.

The good works of the flesh, though so well-pleasing to the carnal mind, tested by God's justice, are at the King's mint adjudged base coin.

Salvation, Justification, Pardon

The salvation of God delivers a man, not only from the guilt, but the dominion of sin, and brings him into fellowship with God. This salvation is preached to "every creature" under heaven; and it leaves without excuse every one who does not receive it.

"What shall I do?" says the sinner. Alas! man *has done* his work completely—the work of self-destruction. Christ has wrought a perfect work—the work of redemption for the salvation of the inexcusably guilty, the utterly lost.

God justifies the sinner believing. When God pardons, He justifies. Man may pardon; he cannot blot out. God alone can justify; and He justifies by Christ, who was made sin for us, that we might be made the righteousness of God in Him.

Had the Lord waited ere He came into this world till men knew their own sickness, then would pride and ignorance have shut Him out for ever.

God, in self-moved love, sent His own Son to save the lost.

The poor sinner, fleeing to Christ for salvation, cannot possibly be overtaken by the sword of the avenger, because that poor sinner is taught by the Spirit of God, and is drawn by God's lovingkindness to the Saviour Christ. Great may be his fear and perplexity; but he is safe from curse in Christ the City of Refuge. God sees him already there, while he himself doubts of reaching it.

"How can I be pardoned?" says the poor self-condemned sinner. "How can I not pardon?" says God. The sinner looks at his sins; but God looks at His Son's atoning blood. Sinner, do thou likewise.

I was slain and hanged on the cross eighteen hundred years ago with Christ (Gal. 2:20). Did He rise? Yes. Therefore I am risen. The Christian is a dead and buried man, and also risen. As a child of Adam, dead and buried; as a child of God, risen with Christ: the world is crucified to him, and he is crucified to the world. Satan ever aims to raise the dead, and bury the living.

God's Wise and Gracious Dealings

If we have especially trusted God in any matter, He will "after these things" (Gen. 22) prove our faith: and though He may seem not to regard us, and that for a long time; yet, in the end, He will show that His way of performing His promise is worthy of Him—good for us.

God's discipline of His children always bears the mark of long-suffering.

When the Lord is about to give great blessings, He commonly begins with great trials. He writes death upon the purposed mercy, that when life springs out of death, we may know from whom that life proceeds—even Jesus, the "I am that I am."

Our peculiar corruptions are often brought out by the peculiarities of others.

If God in His kindness make manifest to ourselves the evil that is in us, it is in order that we may be driven to Christ, and that we may know the subduing power of His blood.

The Lord has bound up the rod of correction in our bundle of blessings.

We have not wisdom to judge of God's ways, unless we have patience to wait their issue.

God is wont to frustrate our devices in order to execute His own purposes, and thereby to do us good to the utmost.

Elisha was singularly honoured after going down to the grave: a dead body touching the prophet's bones came to life again. Elijah was honoured by translation: like Enoch, he did not see death. God will, in manifold wisdom, honour each and every one of them that honour Him.

When God is about to do the very best for us, His discipline is often such that at first our flesh rebels: but let us leave God to bless us in His own way; only let our hearts be set upon Himself, and on pleasing Him. He will be ever true to Himself.

Obedience

"Vain man would be wise, though he be born like a wild ass's colt" (Job 11:12). But God demands it of man that he become a fool, that he may be wise (1 Cor. 3:18).

God honoured the obedience of His saints in time of the old covenant with the abundance of earthly things; if at any time He dealt otherwise, as in Job's case, He departed from His ordinary course. Now the obedience of faith brings with it tribulation, more or less. If we bear not this in mind, trials will often take us by surprise.

The state of the heart of God's children is not to be judged by what they call "comfort," or the lack of it; by strong words or lively feelings; but by steady obedience to His Word—not obedience on great occasions only: it is easier to do great things for Christ than to hold on our way, keeping heart and lips in our every-day walk.

The only path of safety and happiness is prompt, unquestioning obedience to the commandments of the Lord.

If we would be led into God's truth, we must put our neck into Christ's yoke, and in such subjection of spirit as not to be galled thereby.

If you compare a path of obedience with one of disobedience, the great difference may not immediately appear; but years will speak, and show things in their true light.

It is good to bear in mind that whatever our circumstances, it cannot be necessary to disobey God. Let us not wish for anything unless the means to obtain it be as much approved of by God as the *end*.

The "perfect man" is he who has a deliberate purpose to do the will of God in all things, under all circumstances, and at all times; never resting in this or that measure of obedience, but still running the race, his eye fixed on the goal.

Being delivered from the law, we are under obligation to try all our ways, past and present, by the example of the Lord Jesus Christ.

Watchfulness and Self-Denial

"Take no thought for the morrow" (Matt. 6:34)—that is, no *anxious thought*—for this comes of distrust of God. But there is a thought for the morrow which is a holy carefulness: "A prudent man foreseeth the evil, and hideth himself" (Prov. 22:3). Gathering clouds bespeak a coming storm. Watch and be ready for every storm: be it in your own heart, in the church, or in the world, provide against it by abiding in Christ; He is our hiding-place, our high tower into which the righteous runneth and is safe. "Watch ye, and pray, lest ye enter into temptation."[35]

Even when we have most of the consolations of Christ, and most of His approval, let us be on the watch, lest like the spouse in the Song, through the deceitfulness of the flesh, we leave the blessedness of tender communion and put ourselves to shame by "I sleep, but my heart waketh" (Song of Sol. 5:2).

What love to the Thessalonians must Paul have had, who, though he so greatly delighted in his brethren's fellowship, sent Timothy from Athens to Thessalonica, and was content to be left alone!

If a child of God pleases the flesh under colour of liberty, mistaking carnal liberty for spiritual, who can say how far he may go wrong? It is the self-denial of grace that is true liberty.

35. Mark 14:38

Christ measures our kindness to others, especially toward His members, not by the greatness of our gifts, but by our faith and self-denial.

When we see any servant of Christ lowly and self-denying, such we must esteem and revere. To great gifts of knowledge and utterance unaccompanied with lowliness, we pay the tax of admiration; but our esteem and reverence they cannot command.

The habit of denying self in little things will give us a vigour of spiritual life.

In looking out for opportunities of doing great things in the Lord's cause, we lose the daily, hourly opportunities for little acts of self-denial which especially require the grace of Christ. To be crucifying self when no eye but that of God sees us, this is the most acceptable service to our Lord and Master.

That is the best watching and waiting which puts the keeping of our souls into the hands of God; for, "except the Lord keep the city, the watchman waketh but in vain" (Psalm 127:1).

Temptations and Falls

When a mercy comes in the form of affliction, we often need time and grace to call it a mercy: happy they who need not time to do so.

The letter from Hezekiah's enemy drave him to God; whilst that from the flattering king ensnared his feet (2 Kings 19-20).

Some temptations are best withstood by fleeing from them.

We should distinguish between a dead state of soul and a tempted state. Job, in his trouble, was in a tempted state: he says in his sorrow, "Oh that I were as in months past" (Job 29:2). David was in a dead state of soul when he rose from his bed to walk upon the housetop (2 Sam. 11:2). Job felt his temptation: David was not awake to danger.

The devil is often like the practised sharper,[36] who allows his dupes a little success that he may strip them of their all at the last. Thus can Satan suffer his slaves to break off grosser sins, that he may hold them fast bound in the chains of self-righteousness and false peace.

If through confidence in the flesh we take not counsel of God, He is wont to leave us to ourselves, that we may prove our wisdom to be folly. Had Joshua sought counsel of God, he would not have been deceived by the Gibeonites and their tokens of a long journey (Josh. 9).

---

36. Con artist

The evil of the heart is best revealed to God's people by their abiding at the Mercy-seat: if they will not learn there, God may leave them to learn by some gross outbreak. Paul exercised himself to keep always a conscience void of offence, and by constant communion with God well-knew the deceitfulness of the flesh.

If we are found mourning within the vail over inward evil, we shall be preserved from outwardly dishonouring the Lord.

No child of God ever falls at once into the mire of sin. All declension begins in unwatchfulness and neglect of secret dealing with God, whereby Satan finds a door of entrance into the heart, and we are taken in his snares.

Prayer

A child knocks at the father's door with boldness and perseverance, and, knowing the rights of a child, takes no denial. Thus should it be with the children of God, who, through Christ's atonement, have liberty of access to the Father.

Every child of God prays, but not all know what it is to *labour* in prayer (Col. 4:12).

Much prayer for the ungodly is a sign of a thriving soul. Christ prayed for His enemies, "Father, forgive them; for they know not what they do" (Luke 23:34). Paul prayed for the Jews; his "heart's desire and prayer to God for Israel was that they might be saved" (Rom. 10:1). God's precepts (not His decrees) are the rule for our prayers. He would have us pray for all men (1 Tim. 2:1).

To be sustained in faith under long delay of the answer to prayer is itself an answer to prayer beyond price (Matt. 15:22-28).

When we cannot pray at all, then is it high time to pray. We honour God by fighting with inward difficulties, and show our faith in the intercession of the Lord Jesus by bringing our coldness of spirit to the great High Priest.

True boldness in prayer is not to be judged by good words, but by this test: How far is the will of the flesh trodden under foot, and God's will the guide of the soul?

If the ear of sinners be shut to our words, let our mouth be opened at the Mercy-seat in their behalf.

The children of God are apt to think meanly of their prayers and holy things, and to doubt the acceptance of their offerings because of imperfections. It is well indeed to have the humble mind; but unbelief is not pleasing to God. The prattlings of a child are sweeter in the Father's ear than all the best-spoken words of a bond-servant.

Elisha asked for "a hard thing" (2 Kings 2:10). So with many of our requests; they are not things too hard for the Lord, who delights to give liberally, and with whom nothing is impossible: but a prepared heart is needed to receive a great spiritual blessing; and it is by much self-denial the heart is prepared.

Christ's intercession is grounded on His atonement; and so is the prayer of faith.

When we ask for conformity to Christ, and are not content to be stripped and emptied, it is prayer going out of feigned lips (Psalm 15:1).

God our Father can refuse His children nothing that is for their good. Those who have acquaintance with God desire only what is according to His will—they know their happiness lies in having no will but His. Thus they have everything their own way: it is their delight to please God, and what pleases God pleases them.

The prayers recorded in Scripture say much in few words; and the soul persuaded that "God is" cannot be wordy—takes hold of God, and prevails.

Few are strangers to *making* prayers, but how many, alas, are strangers to prayer! The soul in true prayer looks at the cross, and says, Were it not for that cross I should never have prayed at all.

The prayer of the psalmist is often no more than a cry, a sigh, a desire of the poor, the contrite soul.

It is not by our much outward work that the value of our service will be judged in the day of the Lord. Many of the church's best helpers are intercessors confined to their beds.

The importunate widow (Luke 18) represents the whole of God's elect. They are a praying people: and the parable teaches them that God will prove their faith; will seem to the flesh to favour their adversary; but that perseverance in prayer will surely prevail.

The circumstances of every hour furnish us with errands to the throne of grace; and we ought, in the secret of our hearts, to be communing with God our Father all the day long, hearing His voice, asking His guidance, or making confession, if in any of these things we fail. As we advance in acquaintance with God and with ourselves, we shall have more and more of the spirit of *little children*, distrusting ourselves, and putting all our trust in Him.

Answers to Prayer

The best answers to prayer are those we have to wait and trust for. If we are answered quickly, let us be thankful; but let us be assured that by-and-by God will change His method with us, and that we shall be often made to wait.

"I will cry unto God . . . that performeth all things for me" (Psalm 57:2). Every such prayer must be answered; but we must wait God's time and way. The finest fruit of the Spirit ripens the latest; the longer we have to wait for answers to our prayers, the richer the blessing: we are blessed while we continue to pray; faith grows by waiting; the blessing is full when it comes, and the time of the answer is seen to be the right time.

Asking of God what is most precious in His sight, we surely obtain all inferior good. Thus did Solomon (1 Kings 3:6-14). All mercies are bound up with God's gift of Christ.

It is not good for us to obtain deliverance and gifts from God, until we fully justify Him in His way of dealing with us (Psalm 22). The answer to prayer will sometimes come when our patience is spent. "Let patience have her perfect work" (James 1:4), that such rebukes of God's love may not be needful.

Many of God's people pray without waiting for God to work in His own time and manner. Let us not quiet conscience by praying, and then, in fleshly haste, take our own way.

The way wherein it pleases God to answer our prayer, if we have a right mind, will always please us well.

Holiness

As is our faith in Jesus, so will be the holiness of our walk. Where there is much dealing by faith with the blood of atonement, there will be sure and even walking in the path of obedience to the precepts of Christ.

How careful should we be to keep clean the house that is the dwelling of the King of Glory!

Holiness first and pardon after, says the blind Pharisee; but God's way is pardon and peace with God first: holiness the fruit of pardon.

The deep engraving of "Thou art holy" (Psalm 22:3), on the heart of a believer, is necessary to his wise and prudent walk.

Neglected hearts become like dwellings with slovenly occupants—void of comfort.

Every saint is a vessel of mercy, but not every saint a vessel unto honour: yet it is his obligation to be such; lack of obedience gains nothing but harm and loss.

The Secret Life and the Daily Path

The soul that aims high in point of obedience to God will account that a transgression which may not seem to be a fault to the eyes of others.

So soon as we behave and quiet ourselves, and become as a weaned child, our troubles vanish: take away self-will, and the sorrows that remain in our cup are made sweet.

Be much with God in secret, so will you bring profit into the saints' assemblies, and bring profit away from them.

God makes more of the dedication of the heart than of any outward service we can render.

Would you grow up into Christ, make a conscience of obedience to Him in the smallest matters.

Believers should so live and commune in secret with Christ, that all around may see Christ in them.

If we would deal wisely with our daily matters, we must bring God's eternal counsels into them, and consider their eternal issues; holding ourselves God's servants, doing each his part in preparing the way for the Lord's appearing in glory.

The path for a believer to walk in without stumbling is that of God's precepts; in treading which he keeps his conscience purged by the blood of Christ, takes up his cross daily, and denies himself. This path, alas, is not much trodden by the saints—to the unregenerate utterly unknown.

Do you dread to grieve the heart of Christ, as you once dreaded wrath and condemnation?

The Day of Small Things

God never blames us for our slow progress and small attainments in holiness, but for our sluggish cold-hearted submitting to evil and allowing it dominion over us.

Even our purposes to do right are made much of by our gracious and pitiful God: therefore let us not despise the desires of our hearts to please Him.

If we watch against pride; if we struggle and pray against it; if we are pained at its inward workings—then that which we feel to be only a struggle after humility, God accounts humility true and deep. He accepts us in His dear Son: He accepts our offerings also; and the sighs of the contrite He calls incense.

The Believer's Testimony to Others

Let me not consider what I have as mine own; for I myself am not mine own. Whatever I have, therefore—talents, substance—I am God's steward to use all at His bidding, for His glory.

The guilt of sin was not revealed to saints of Old Testament time as now to us. Christ, that was to come, was dimly seen by them: Christ, who has come, is fully revealed to us. Obligations are according to revelation.

This world is but a desert—a foreign land, where the children of God can find no rest: if, through unbelief, they seek it, they will only find disappointment.

We ought so to behave ourselves, that the ungodly may see the mind of Christ in all our ways; even look and voice should bear witness for Christ: "Ye are My witnesses" (Isa. 43:10).

One word spoken with a savour of Christ may sink into the soul of the hearer and bring forth fruit unto eternal life.

There is something in the very countenance of those who walk with God that gives authority to all they say.

Happiness, Joy, Comfort, and Peace

All our wounds are for Christ's binding up: our broken hearts become witnesses to His skill and loving-kindness; for it is spoken by the prophet, "Himself took our infirmities, and bare our sicknesses" (Matt. 8:17).

Special comfort and consolation may be given to any Christian; but it is the diligence of the soul in walking with God that brings settled comfort.

Consolation in Jesus will abound as our sorrow for sin is deep, and our desire for obedience sincere.

If our peace be marred amidst our upright desires to please the Lord, it is because of self-willed purposes mingled with those upright desires.

We speak of our comfort and peace being marred by the ways of others towards us, little considering that self-will is the author of our vexation.

It is our duty to be always happy. True, we may be sorrowful; but if we be unhappy, it is because we have been drinking of some foul stream, and not of our fountain of joy—God Himself.

A happy, joyful spirit spreads joy everywhere; a fretful spirit is a trouble to ourselves, and to all around us.

Let us solemnly consider how much we may injure others when we are fretful and willful, and how much we may help others when we are joyful in God.

If God impart to us peculiar joy in the Holy Ghost, filling us with Christ and His love, causing us to keep holy Sabbath in the soul by faith of Jesus, it is for this end—that we may come down from the mount to do the work of the Lord, ready to bear all things for Jesus' sake.

If any believer lack peace and joy, let him examine himself by the Word, and use diligence in cleansing heart and conscience by the blood of Jesus.

The joy of the Holy Ghost is a holy, solemn thing. It always humbles the soul, and keeps it low. Not so the joy of the flesh.

Begin every day with the Word of God and prayer, if you would enjoy settled blessedness. It is in the Word of God that the fulness of Christ is revealed, as the rich portion of every one who trusts in the blood of Christ.

The peace of the believer, through faith in the atoning blood of Jesus, if the soul be flourishing, flows like a river; *joy* in believing is the same river overflowing its banks. Let watchfulness keep pace with joy.

Church Discipline

The discipline exercised by the church of God should be a picture of our heavenly Father's character.

A sober mind, a tender heart, a watchful spirit, should mark those who put away the evil doer.

All God's corrections and judgments are designed to bring to repentance. So likewise any censure pronounced by an assembly of saints, while manifestly righteous, should be as medicine to restore, that the spirit may be saved in the day of Christ (l Cor. 5:5).

Paul says not to the Corinthians, when he reproves their evil, "lest my God should humble *you*," but "lest my God should humble *me* among you"; not "lest I should be wrathful and cut off many," but lest I should "bewail many which have sinned" (2 Cor. 12:21).

My brother, defiling himself, is my own hand touching pitch. In this mind we are like Christ, who is touched with the feeling of our infirmities, and is able to succour the tempted.

In how many instances, alas! where sharp or bitter reproof is given, heavenly wisdom would deal in tender-hearted counsel and admonition.

Colossians 4:10 is a testimony that Mark was restored and stablished after having forsaken Paul and Barnabas. We find him not with Barnabas, but with Paul, who had so gravely judged his fault. "Rebuke a wise man, and he will love thee" (Prov. 9:8).

Let us imitate our Lord in His pity toward those who have erred from His way; thus we best discountenance their sins, and help them to make the confession that obtains forgiveness from God. Carnal severity hardens the heart which might be won by heavenly tenderness and compassion.

In the fellowship of saints' assemblies are many joys and many comforts. It is not, however, a bed of roses; for it is in the intercourse of that fellowship that the infirmities and faults of believers especially appear. In the church's best state there was always the flesh to be subdued, and Satan resisted. Hence "forbearing one another, and forgiving one another, if any man have a quarrel against any: even as Christ forgave you, even also do ye" (Col. 3:13).

Judgments of offences should be such as to commend themselves to the common conscience. All are accountable to God for those judgments.

The love of Christ filling our hearts, we shall be keen-sighted to discern, whether in ourselves or others, whatsoever pleases not the Lord. This love, and this love only, will enable us to maintain the order and discipline of the house of God, so as to be approved by the Son of God, the Lord of His own house. We shall thereby, while observing the laws of Christ as to offending brethren, be raised above the fear of man that bringeth a snare; and, what is higher still, be free of false love, which spares the rod when God would have us smite. "Let the righteous smite me; it shall be a kindness" (Psalm 141:5). "Faithful are the wounds of a friend" (Prov. 27:6).

The Servants of the Lord

Whatever carnal titles of honour men may give to professed ministers of the gospel, the conscience of the unregenerate will not account them holy men of God unless they be such of a truth.

For those who are to exercise any office in the church—that of evangelist, pastor—it is not knowledge and utterance only which are needed; but also, and above all, grace and an unblameable conversation.[37] Whilst they be harmless as doves in regard to carnal policy, they should be wise as serpents in respect of spiritual wisdom and prudence, so as to "cut off occasion from them which desire occasion" (2 Cor. 11:12).

It was a small thing with Paul to be judged by the saints at Corinth. Whatever their judgments, he is intent on doing them good, and holds on his course, glorifying God. He labours to restore them to a sound heart and mind. "We do all things, dearly beloved, for your edifying. For I fear lest, when I come, I shall not find you such as I would" (2 Cor. 12:19-20).

The servant of the Lord Jesus must be instant in season and out of season, knowing that he is the Lord's messenger to every one with whom he has to do: ever learning of the Lord; for, seeing that he is to be continually ministering to others, he must be

37. i.e., way of life

receiving fresh supplies from the God of all grace through all channels. Meditation of the Word and prayer should occupy the chief part of his time. In his public ministry and private conversation, he should aim at heart and conscience, seeking in every way to magnify Christ and abase the creature. In short, he should set the Lord always before him, and so walk in His steps as to represent Him to every eye.

If Paul had much joy in his spiritual children at Philippi, he had much profit, though little joy, by those at Corinth, who by their many evils gave him so great occasion to show the heart of Christ.

Those who walk with God hear His voice, and He employs them.

A good workman gains skill by his mistakes.

The Lord Jesus always finds service for willing hearts and willing hands: let us desire only that service for which He has fitted us.

If each child of God, each member of Christ, had due conscience of his own accountability, we should soon see better things in the church of God. If we be careless in the Lord's service, He will surely require it of us.

Let the servants of Christ put toil and hardship by the side of the recompense, and look well to the state of their hearts, taking heed day by day that they please God: so will they be always rejoicing, though always sorrowful.

The joy and triumph of faith are only to be found in the way of unreserved consecration of ourselves to God, and of diligent service of Christ.

All who labour for Christ shall receive great wages for little toil.

It is our wisdom to account the pleasing God our great reward. If we leave it altogether to His will how and when to give us fruit of our labour, we shall obtain abundantly what, as our chief aim, we do not seek.

Martha would please the Lord in her own way; Mary in her Lord's way. There are many who would please the Lord; but in their own way, for lack of trying their works by the Scriptures: amid much labour they are unspiritual and barren.

From the charge of Paul to Timothy (1 Tim. 4:12-16), we gather the true and proper character of the servant of God.[38]

The work of a servant of the Lord demands entire self-denial. "Even Christ pleased not Himself" (Rom. 15:3). He must be the servant of all men for Jesus' sake, that he may be, under his Lord, a leader and a commander of the people: the foremost to suffer; the most laborious in all service; ever caring for others, ever forgetting himself.

---

38. "Let no man despise thy youth; but be thou an example of the believers, in word, in conversation, in charity, in spirit, in faith, in purity. Till I come, give attendance to reading, to exhortation, to doctrine. Neglect not the gift that is in thee, which was given thee by prophecy, with the laying on of the hands of the presbytery. Meditate upon these things; give thyself wholly to them; that thy profiting may appear to all. Take heed unto thyself, and unto the doctrine; continue in them: for in doing this thou shalt both save thyself, and them that hear thee."

Spiritual Warfare

The children of God in their spiritual warfare too much resemble the children of Israel after Joshua fell asleep (Judges 3:5-8). They did not cast out the remnants of the Canaanites, but made a league with them: so, alas! we have allowed remnants of evil things to hold peaceable possession of corners of our hearts; and, through lack of diligence in weeding the soul's garden, God is but little with us. We have neglected to take the foxes, the little foxes, which spoil the vines (Song of Sol. 2:15).

There were four things which made Israel fight well under Joshua: first, the necessity of fighting; second, the certainty of victory; third, God with them; and fourth, the rich spoil. How is it that God's people, with Christ for their Captain, are but sorry soldiers?

If Christ be with us, what is the city of strength, what are the walls of Jericho, but an occasion to faith (Josh. 6)?

The slothful believer may have trouble through the flesh; but he never knows the evil and power of the flesh as do those who fight against it and subdue it.

God's Deeper Dealings

Witness for Christ lies in self-condemnation according to the rule of the Word of God. Sinners are as many as the race of Adam; but a poor and needy sinner is a precious jewel in the sight of Christ.

We are not to gather from the angel's feeding Elijah that God approved of his going to Horeb (1 Kings 19). If God gives us good things when we are out of the way, we ought to see keen reproof in His very kindness.

God will put His faithful servants into the furnace to prove them and fit them for honour (Gen. 39). Joseph was steadfast in obedience to God, and true to Potiphar in all things; yet his service to Potiphar ended in bonds and dishonour. Joseph in prison seemed forgotten of God; but God was faithful, and raised His faithful servant to promised honour, after fitting him for that honour by humiliation and suffering.

The cross of Christ brought in a new order of faith, so that now the children of God, when walking in obedience and simplicity of heart before God, should expect trials of faith like those of Christ. Did they settle this in their hearts, they would not be surprised at God's giving them to drink of Christ's cup, and to share His baptism: they would suffer gladly, remembering that the curse of the law cannot touch them.

If we walk in self-will and unbelief, the holy rebukes of the still small voice of the Spirit will not be heard; but if our hearts are *listening*, God will be ever teaching us by ways innumerable—chiefly by the Holy Scriptures.

Pleasing the Lord

A wish of David's was a law to his three mighty men (2 Sam. 23:15-16). Should not then a wish of Christ's be a law to us? Shall Christ have one mind; and we, His flesh and bones, another? With this tender mind toward our Lord, we shall follow hard after Him, and pursue nothing that may bring shame upon us.

Oh, let us think of the tenderness of the heart of Christ! No apple of the eye so tender as that heart. Let us then be careful to do His will; chiefly lest we grieve Him; but also for our own comfort and joy.

A child of God ought to be ever committing himself into God's hand, that God may direct his way for him. The natural man deviseth his own way; but God would have His children hang upon Him for counsel and guidance in everything.

One of David's mighty men fought single-handed with the Philistine host for a piece of ground full of lentils: others might have thought it not worth fighting for, but it was parcel of king David's land; and to his faithful one that was enough. Let us in our spiritual warfare be like that good soldier (2 Sam. 23:11-12).[39]

Be content, for He hath said, "I will never leave thee, nor forsake thee." This promise was first given to Jacob; then to Joshua:

---

39. "And after him was Shammah the son of Agee the Hararite. And the Philistines were gathered together into a troop, where was a piece of ground full of lentiles: and the people fled from the Philistines. But he stood in the midst of the ground, and defended it, and slew the Philistines: and the Lord wrought a great victory."

now it is spoken to all God's children (Gen. 28:15; Josh. 1:5; Heb. 13:5). Let me lay up this promise in my heart, and I am a rich man. How can I please God today? He will take care of tomorrow, will be my settled, blessed mind.

Providences

Never judge God by His providence, unless your will is wholly subject to His will. To judge Him before the issue of His dealings is to judge rashly and wrongly. The end of the Lord will justify all His ways. When Job rashly judged, he said, "Thou art become cruel to me"; but at last he justified God, saying, "Behold, I am vile." "I abhor myself" (Job 30:21; 40:4; 42:6).

Let us put all our matters into God's hands, and leave them there. Can they be better ordered than by Him? We never think that the sun, moon, and stars will go wrong, because man has nothing to do with the ordering of them.

Be familiar with this precious thought, that God decrees the little as well as the great things of His providence; and that all His decrees are those of love to His people.

Gratitude

Mercies reviewed and pondered are even sweeter than when first bestowed.

Amongst the perilous mercies pleasing to nature is health of body. Sickness, although a mark of the curse, usually favours, more than health, communion with God.

True gratitude never says, I have done enough.

The best way to keep our mercies is to be ready at all times to give them up at God's call.

A child of God, taking a cup of cold water with a thankful heart, may render a better service to God than one who gives thousands of gold and silver.

Ingratitude towards God for benefits received makes us distrustful of Him as to the future.

Praise

Praising God should be to us our chiefest, happiest employ. It is the "service of song" of the sanctuary.

God preserve us from ingratitude, that abominable thing, that viper which creeps forth when the sun is up; for when signal mercies demand especial thankfulness, how often have we resembled Hezekiah, who rendered not again according to the benefit (2 Chron. 32:25).

To hang my harp upon the willows is to say, "Christ is not ruling well."

So long as our hearts are cleaving to earthly things, we shall not be able to sing the pilgrim's song; but if we are thorough pilgrims, and apprehend our great High Priest ever living for us at the right hand of God, we shall be perpetually giving thanks.

Can I fail to praise God *always for all things*, if I have no interests but the interests of Christ, and no purposes but those of Christ? Let me, by faith, but see Christ at the right hand of God ordering all things by His wisdom as the head of the body the church (Eph. 1:22-23; 5:23), I shall then see Him prospering in all that He doeth, and with Him I shall ever rejoice.

To avoid an unthankful spirit, we must make thankfulness a business.

If we thank God for *wants*, we shall not distrust Him for *supplies*.

If, because of painful circumstances, we cannot praise the Lord, we ought to confess the sin (Eph. 5:20).[40]

---

40. "Giving thanks always for all things unto God and the Father in the name of our Lord Jesus Christ . . . "

I would especially urge it upon the people of God to maintain a *good conscience* and a *thankful heart*.

Look back on the last seven days of your life: how much of thanksgiving and praise has your heart rendered to God?

Communion with God, by hearkening to His voice in the Scriptures, and speaking with Him in praise and prayer by the Spirit of His Son, each member of Christ fulfilling his own office, is the proper end of every assembly of saints.

Oh that we were wise and tender-hearted, to cease from grieving that Holy Spirit of promise, our indwelling Paraclete! Then would the comfort of love, and fellowship of the Spirit, in every assembly, be earnest and foretaste of our perfect fellowship at the coming of the Lord.

"Behold, I come quickly; and My reward is with Me, *to give every man according as his work shall be*" (Rev. 22:12).

"If ye keep My commandments, ye shall abide in My love [that is, in the communion of My love]; even as I have kept My Father's commandments, and abide in His love" (John 15:10).

"Ye are My friends, if ye do *whatsoever* I command you" (John 15:14).

"Abide in Me, and I in you" (John 15:4).

"He that eateth My flesh, and drinketh My blood, dwelleth [or abideth] in Me, and I in him" (John 6:56).

Topical Index

Answers to Prayer *127*
Believer's Testimony to Others, The *131*
Calling of the Church, The *50*
Cares *84*
Character *81*
Chastisement *85*
Christ *37*
Christ and the Church *39*
Christian Communion *104*
Christ's Example *44*
Christian's Walk, The *93*
Church Discipline *134*
Circumstances *75*
Coming of the Lord, The *59*
Communion with God *32*
Confession of Sin *14*
Conflict *63*
Conscience *17*
Cross of Christ, The *20*
Danger and Temptations *92*
Day of Small Things, The *130*
Dealing with the Faults of Others *97*
Deep and Silent Work *100*
Discipline *87*
Evil Passions *70*
Evil Speaking *99*
Experience *90*

Faith *27*
Forgiveness *67*
Form of Godliness, The *113*
Fruit *103*
God's Deeper Dealings *140*
God's Wise and Gracious Dealings *116*
Gospel, The *1*
Gratitude *144*
Happiness, Joy, Comfort, and Peace *132*
Heart and Its Deceitfulness, The *111*
Holiness *128*
Holy Spirit, The *43*
Human Nature *24*
Humility and Self-Abasement *73*
Justice and Judgment *109*
Law and the Gospel, The *3*
Little Things *102*
Love *107*
Love of God, The *110*
Natural Man and His Religion, The *8*
"New Creature," The *53*
Obedience *82, 118*
Pleasing the Lord *141*
Poverty of Spirit *68*
Praise *145*

Prayer *60, 124*
Providences *143*
Salvation, Justification, Pardon *114*
Scriptures, The *5*
Secret Life and the Daily Path, The *129*
Self-Knowledge and Self-Judgment *71*
Servants of the Lord, The *136*
Service *64*
Service to Christ *66*
Sin *10*
Sins of Believers, The *56*
Sound Mind, A *91*
Spiritual Warfare *139*
Strength and Continuance *78*
Temptations and Falls *122*
Trial of Faith, The *45*
Trial of the Servants of Christ *96*
Unbelief *54*
Watchfulness and Self-Denial *120*

www.ingramcontent.com/pod-product-compliance
Lightning Source LLC
Chambersburg PA
CBHW052047070526
44584CB00017B/2089